A STUDY OF COST ANALYSIS IN HIGHER EDUCATION

Volume 2:

THE PRODUCTION AND USE OF COST ANALYSIS IN INSTITUTIONS OF HIGHER EDUCATION

CARL R. ADAMS
RUSSELL L. HANKINS
GORDON W. KINGSTON
ROGER G. SCHROEDER

Department of Management Sciences
Graduate School of Business Administration
University of Minnesota

AMERICAN COUNCIL ON EDUCATION, Washington, D.C.

A STUDY OF COST ANALYSIS IN HIGHER EDUCATION
ISBN for complete set: 0-8268-1431-X
Titles in the set are listed in the Foreword
  to each of the four volumes.

Library of Congress Cataloging in Publication Data

Main entry under title: *CI*   JUN 1 8 1979

The production and use of cost analysis in institutions
    of higher education.

    (A Study of cost analysis in higher education ; v. 2
    Bibliography: p.
    1. Education, Higher--United States--Costs.
2. Educational surveys--United States. 3. Educational accountability--United States. I. Adams, Carl R
II. Series.
LB2342.S87 vol. 2   379'.1214'0973s [379'.1214'0973]
                                              78-1779

9 8 7 6 5 4 3 2 1

Printed in the United States of America

FOREWORD

The American Council on Education's Office of Administrative Affairs initiated during 1974 a series of studies of the financial condition of higher education, partly in response to certain recommendations in the final report of the National Commission on the Financing of Postsecondary Education. One recommendation proposed that "interim national standard procedures for calculating...costs per student should be adopted by the federal government..."--a recommendation reflecting the assumption that "the most useful unit cost data for administrators and policy makers are the...annual per-student costs of instruction for each major field of study, level of instruction, and type of institution." [1] This assumption and the related proposal seemed to the American Council on Education to be insufficiently grounded in tested methodology and empirical evidence. Fearing adverse institutional consequences of premature implementation, the Council in the spring of 1974 requested and received a grant from the Ford Foundation for a systematic investigation of the varied concepts, procedures, uses, and outcomes of cost analysis in higher education.

The proposed studies were conducted at the University of Minnesota (Department of Management Sciences, Graduate School of Business Administration) under a contract with the American Council on Education. Carl R. Adams served as project director, and his collaborators were Roger G. Schroeder, Russell L. Hankins, and Gordon W. Kingston. Reports of their work are being published in four volumes, under the title A Study of Cost

_____
1. Financing Postsecondary Education in the United States (Washington: Government Printing Office, 1973), pp. 340, 339.

iii

Analysis in Higher Education, with volume titles as follows: Volume 1,
The Literature of Cost and Cost Analysis in Higher Education (Adams, Hankins,
Schroeder); Volume 2, The Production and Use of Cost Analysis in Institu-
tions of Higher Education (Adams, Hankins, Kingston, Schroeder); Volume 3,
Site Visit Descriptions of Costing Systems and Their Use in Higher Education
(edited by Schroeder); Volume 4, The Future Use of Cost Analysis in Higher
Education (Adams, Kingston, Schroeder).

Detailed presentations of procedures, results, and conclusions were
judged to be desirable in these reports, partly because of the dearth of
such information in prior literature in this field. In particular, it was
believed that relatively full documentation would greatly improve the
scholarly foundations for future research and development in institutional
administration. Moreover, the concrete descriptions and critical evaluations of institutional experience with cost analysis seemed likely to encourage more discriminating use of this methodology in future administrative
applications.

A critical turning point in the economy of higher education occurred
in 1973-74--as it did for the entire nation. Partly because of the oil
embargo, that year brought to crisis proportions the combined effects of
cost inflation and income recession. Although colleges and universities
had been grappling for several years with the effects of declining enrollment growth and lagging income, the retrenchments required by the new
conditions were unprecedented in order of magnitude. Inasmuch as the work
of the Minnesota investigators began in July 1974, they were afforded an
unusual opportunity over the following two years to study representative

institutions in the process of making these difficult adjustments and to appraise the utility of cost analysis as an administrative tool. Their observations and analyses should provide insight into the managerial behavior of the period and valuable guidance to higher education administrators seeking to improve future decisions concerning the allocation and use of institutional resources.

More generally, the methodology, results, interpretations, and conclusions recorded in these four volumes comprise a rich store of conceptual and empirical knowledge which should greatly advance the study of administration in higher education toward the mainstream of the decision sciences.

Lyle H. Lanier, Director (1972-76)
Office of Administrative Affairs
American Council on Education

The American Council on Education is pleased to issue the four-volume study of cost analysis in higher education for the benefit of college and university administrators and others concerned with cost determination in institutions of higher education. The initial conception for the study was largely that of Lyle H. Lanier, then director of the Council's Office of Administrative Affairs, and the Council is indebted to him for his competence, professional interest, and leadership. The authors have ably pursued a thoroughgoing investigation to present materials that should help improve institutional cost analyses and resource allocations. In the interests of time and economy, the reports are published, without further editing, as submitted. The Council wishes especially to acknowledge the grant from the Ford Foundation which made the project possible.

J. W. Peltason, President
American Council on Education

PREFACE

In late 1973 and early 1974 there was considerable national interest in output-related instructional costs. As a result, the American Council on Education (ACE) undertook an evaluation of the current use and utility of cost analysis in higher education institutions. Because the ACE constituency is largely institutional and because of the general lack of documentation in this area, the study was designed to focus primarily on the institutional perspective. Funding for this over two-year investigation was provided through a grant from the Ford Foundation. Both ACE and the Ford Foundation thought that the study should be undertaken as an independent research project. As a result, the College of Business Administration at the University of Minnesota received a contract for major phases of the project.

The principal tasks undertaken by the project staff at the University of Minnesota included a documentation of the experience of representative higher education institutions in producing cost information and an assessment of the usefulness of cost information in administrative decision processes. The study provides an evaluation of currently available instructional cost data, the techniques currently employed in the translation of cost data into meaningful information and the desired cost information to support administrative decision processes. An additional perspective is created by the investigation of anticipated future developments in costing and cost analysis through use of the Delphi technique.

Four major reports have resulted from the research conducted at the University of Minnesota. Monograph 1 is a survey of the literature of cost analysis in higher education. Monograph 2 (this monograph) contains the compilation and analysis of data gathered on-site at twenty-one higher education institutions and at various higher education offices in six states and from the responses to questionnaires mailed to 481 institutions. A third volume contains the narrative reports of seventeen of the on-site "case studies" of institutions plus descriptions based on interviews with various higher education offices in four states. Monograph 4 is a report on the Delphi investigation of the expectations for the future technology and impact of cost analysis.

The authors have benefited from the assistance of others in the preparation of this volume. Peter de Janosi, Officer in Charge of Higher Education Research for the Ford Foundation has served as the contact with that agency. Lyle Lanier, Director of the Office of Administrative Affairs and Educational Statistics for the American Council on Education, has provided continued support and constructive criticism. The members of our advisory committee, Raymond Bacchetti, Frederick Balderston, George Chambers, Earl Cheit, John Folger, John Green and Hans Jenny, have given generously of their time and provided valuable insights. Project consultants, David Berg, James Farmer, Mel Orwig, Don Ricketts, Bernard Sheehan, James Topping, and Robert Wallhaus, have helped us see our way through the many problems of design and execution. We have benefited greatly from the collective wisdom of both groups, but we alone bear the responsibility for the content of this volume.

Much of the analysis and presentation of the data dealing with the production of cost information (Chapter 4) was done by Roger Schroeder. The analysis and presentation of the data on cost data availability (Chapter 3) and the institutional use of cost information (Chapter 5) were provided by Carl Adams along with the leadership in preparing the overall general observations (Chapter 6). Russ Hankins and Craig Bickel, our research assistant, were instrumental in putting the mail survey data in machine readable form and preparing data tabulations. Paul Alper, Thomas Hoffmann and Ronald Wenger assisted in the collection of the on-site data. The entire volume benefited from the combined efforts of the authors.

Finally, but by no means least, we acknowledge a debt to our typists, Kathryn Balasingam, who typed our early drafts and Diane Berube who typed the final draft.

TABLE OF CONTENTS

Chapter

APPENDICES

CHAPTER 1.0

INTRODUCTION

1.1 <u>Monograph Purpose</u>

Within the overall project purpose of describing the use and utility of cost information in academic administration, this monograph is the keystone. Its aim is to present and analyze data collected from administrators and information systems specialists in colleges and universities regarding the current use and usefulness of cost information. Whereas the first monograph developed by the project deals with the past and the history of costing and cost analysis and the fourth monograph deals with the future technology and use of cost information, this monograph describes the present both in terms of what cost information is currently being used and its utility in supporting administrative processes.

Along with evaluating the cost information itself we also review recent experience with various aspects of producing cost information. The past ten years have seen significant developmental efforts in the area of information systems both the standard transportable models as well as tailored and home-made versions. Without a well structured investigation of the experiences with these systems development efforts, our main impressions about them are formed from listening to a relatively small set of "war stories." Frequently, these stories are not balanced objective presentations since their presenters tend to be either the heroes or the victims. We have attempted to assess systems experience in as objective and representative a manner as possible.

1

In thinking of the monograph purpose, we might informatively ask, who is the monograph written for and what impact can be expected from reading it? Naturally, the authors viewed the objective of evaluation as requiring the accumulation and analysis of data. Because it presents a considerable amount of the collected data and the data analysis, the monograph should appeal primarily to serious students of academic administration. Still the observations and conclusions developed by the authors should be of interest and value to administrators trying to determine their institutions' posture regarding cost information, to information systems specialists attempting to understand administrative information needs and choose efficient systems approaches to meet them, to state and federal policy makers in appreciating the position of institutions regarding the production and use of cost information, and to serious students of academic administration trying to identify the needs and priorities for future research.

1.2 Scope and General Approach

Cost analysis and cost information in higher education is a large field of study that has been actively researched for more than seventy years. In order to meet its objectives, the Study of Cost Analysis in Higher Education project team had to limit the scope of its interest. During the last five years, much of the attention in higher education costing has focused on state and federal needs for cost information. Because of this and because of the natural interests of the American Council on Education, the project has narrowed the scope of its investigations to cost information and cost analysis techniques intended to supply institutional administrators with the cost data needed for informed, rational decision making. Thus, for example, the use of cost data in macro educational planning and financing is not addressed in the research reported in this monograph. Also, the areas of opportunity costs and societal and individual "out of pocket" costs though sometimes very important are not addressed in this review. Our investigation is limited to costs that are reflected in the financial records of the institution. Another kind of limitation on our investigation is its principal focus of interest on the instructional area although this is not exclusive. Within this narrowed scope, the project team developed an approach for collecting the data necessary to support its evaluative efforts.

Several factors were important in selecting the general approach to use in collecting data. First, there is an issue of which population to sample and represent. On the one hand many institutions have only limited knowledge and experience with the production and use of cost information. Such institutions cannot provide much insight regarding cost information because they simply haven't given it much consideration. Any serious attempt to define a population of experienced institutions would result in a group that includes only 20 to 50 per cent of the approximately 2500 higher education institutions in the country. The 20 per cent level would be the more likely level if experience with the commonly known costing systems such as RRPM, IEP, CAMPUS, SEARCH and PLANTRAN was a criteria. On the other hand there is certainly merit in being able to provide data that adequately represents all of higher education.

A second consideration is the appropriate depth of the inquiry undertaken within sample institutions. The inquiry could range from an extensive on-site study to a relatively simple mail survey. Obviously when you are trying to understand issues of use, utility and experience with systems, it is desirable to provide more depth than is possible with a mail survey approach. Still, the resources required by an extensive case study approach such as that reported by Benacerraf, et al. [1972] for Princeton are prohibitive.

Thirdly, the identification of the respondents in any data gathering as users of information (decision makers) or producers of information (staff) may be important. As the literature review in Monograph 1 suggests there may be a significant disparity in the views of these two groups regarding the use and utility of cost information.

A fourth consideration is the extent to which the institutional perspective is determined by the state agencies dealing with higher education. Understanding the institutional perspective on the use and utility of cost information may require some understanding of the state requirements on the institutions for cost data. Obviously, the study cannot undertake to fully understand the workings of the various types of state offices in the area of higher education. Still, some insight into what types and amounts of cost information requirements these offices perceive is an important factor.

All of the above considerations affected the general approach chosen for collecting data for the study. All of the institutional data collection was segmented into a producer/user dichotomy. Mostly this provides the different perspectives on non-overlapping areas of inquiry. Where the data collection did intentionally overlap, the comparison of the responses of the two groups is interesting. A relatively complete investigation of experienced institutions was provided through on-site interviews over a several day period at each of twenty-one institutions. The institutions visited were chosen from among the set of institutions having experience with costing systems to include schools of all types and sizes. Representativeness for all of higher education was obtained on a limited number of topics through a mail survey sent to almost 500 of the country's 2500 colleges and universities. Some coverage of the state agency impact on institutional use of cost information was provided through on-site interviews with all appropriate agencies (legislative, executive and coordinating) in six states. The states visited have a reputation for activity in the use of cost analysis and each contained some of the institutions that were visited.

By combining the in-depth, mail survey, state office, and producer/ user separation concepts we hope to provide a complete look at the institutional use and utility of cost information.

1.3 Basic Definitions and Framework

The project's first monograph [Adams, Hankins, and Schroeder, 1977] devoted a chapter to basic definitions and concepts. Such material is necessarily somewhat complicated and somewhat tedious and need not be repeated here. Suffice it to say that we are concerning ourselves with the financial accounting definitions of cost. Thus, cost is "the amount or equivalent paid or charged for something of value" (page 13). A wide variety of types of cost can be defined in terms of the characteristics described in Monograph 1. We think of cost analysis as "any manipulation of cost data that is done to provide relevant information for those who make decisions" (page 21). Monograph 1 identifies standard types of analysis including composition analysis, relational analysis, and direct comparisons. Also, we recognize several common approaches to cost analysis including, full cost analysis, breakeven analysis, controllable cost analysis, and comparative analysis. These terms and definitions are incorporated into the data collection activity and the presentation of the resulting data but their effect is not transparent without reading Monograph 1. On the other hand, the basic framework presented in the first monograph as a structure for discussion is clearly the basis for the structure of the data collection and the presentation of the data analysis.

Since the primary purpose of the study is to evaluate the use and utility of cost information it seems logical to structure the data collection and presentation in terms of the administrative processes that are performed in higher education institutions. Monograph 1 describes the administrative processes structure that we have developed. Briefly, the four major categories of processes are: resource acquisition, resource allocation, management and control, and accountability. In the category of resource acquisition are such processes as: tuition setting, resource requirements estimation, and indirect cost recovery rate setting. Resource allocation includes such processes as: programmatic allocation and organizational unit allocation. Within the resource management and control category we include such processes as comparison of expenditures with budget allocations and comparison of expenditures with standard expenditure rates. The category of accountability includes subprocesses that deal with general constituencies on the one hand and with specific supporters on the other.

This structure of administrative processes is reflected in the interview guides prepared for the on-site visits to institutions and state agencies as well as in the mail survey instruments addressed to administrators. As will be further described below, the administrative process structure is also used in presenting the analysis and findings of the study regarding the use and utility of cost information.

1.4 Structure of the Monograph

The remainder of the monograph is structured to present the analysis of the data collected through the site visits and surveys and the observations the authors have made after reviewing the collected data. Chapter 2 provides the details of the data collection design. This includes a discussion of the overall data collection strategy as well as a specification of the sample and the data collection instruments for the institutional site visits, the state agency site visits, and the mail survey.

In Chapter 3 a limited picture of the state of institutional databases related to costing is presented. The data used for this chapter comes primarily from the mail survey so its scope is necessarily limited. Areas of data that are addressed include student activity data, faculty activity and load data, and data related to cost and efficiency measurement.

An analysis of experiences reported in the production of cost information is discussed in Chapter 4. The production systems covered in the chapter are the commonly known models, CAMPUS, RRPM, PLANTRAN, and SEARCH as well as a variety of homemade systems. Various aspects of the systems experience are considered including reviews of the major steps in system development i.e., system selection, development and installation of the system, and system operation. Also, the results or performance of the system operation are evaluated and the area of system costs is discussed. All of the discussion and presentation combines to provide a general evaluation of the experience of the institution with the production of cost information.

Chapter 5 contains a discussion of the data collected on institutional use and utility of cost information. In analyzing data from both the on-site interviews and the mail survey, the discussion is structured according to the major administrative processes categories, i.e., acquisition of funds, allocation of available resources, management and control, and accountability. Obviously some important topics transcend these administrative process categories. Thus, in addition to the discussion of use in terms of these major processes, two special topics are reviewed, namely, state and federal mandated reporting and the area of information exchange.

The final chapter, Chapter 6, is a summary of the observations related to data availability and the production and use of cost information. In addition, some overall observations and conclusions are discussed. The breadth and number of issues and areas addressed by the study necessarily means that the observations and conclusions are to some degree speculative. Nevertheless, they represent our best informed judgment and thus perhaps the best informed judgment currently available.

1.5 Summary of Observations and Conclusions

Careful consideration of the data presented in Chapters 3, 4, and 5 has led us to make a number of observations and to develop some conclusions. These observations and conclusions are discussed at greater length in Chapter 6 but are summarized below for convenience. To facilitate their review, the observations and conclusions are categorized in terms of their relationship to data availability, production of costing, and use of cost information. A category of overall observations and conclusions is also included.

1.5.1 Data Availability

1. Many institutions do not have their data even partially in machine readable form. Most institutions do not have faculty data in machine readable form. Computer system development will be impeded by this problem.

2. Among all institutions there is a relatively low availability of student data by major or degree. Institutions show little interest in programmatic data.

3. Integration of files is a significant problem for almost all institutions.

4. Marginal cost data is almost non-existent in all types of institutions but administrators express a need for its development.

1.5.2 The Production of Cost Information

1. Homemade systems provide greater perceived benefits than vendor supplied systems for internal decision making.

2. For financial projection highly aggregated systems tend to be more useful than the more disaggregated RRPM and CAMPUS systems.

3. Only half the attempted implementations of RRPM or IEP provided useful information.

4. Institutions should identify specific needs and uses for systems prior to system development.

5. Administrators should recognize that it is difficult or impossible to meet internal and external needs for data with the same system.

6. An evolutionary top-down approach to the development of cost information systems should be followed.

1.5.3 Institutional Use of Cost Information

1. Cost data and analysis is important in institutional decision making but it is not a dominant consideration.

2. Knowledge of cost related data (e.g. class sizes, student/faculty ratios, faculty workloads) is preferred to unit cost data both in internal decision processes and for exchange of data with other institutions.

3. While institutions show considerable support for the exchange of cost and cost related data, they have major concerns regarding the techniques used and the selection of institutions for comparison.

4. Institutions are far more interested in submitting cost data by level and discipline than in programmatic categories.

5. Very little cost analysis is used in managerial control activities.

6. Many institutions, particularly the major research ones, indicate that NCHEMS IEP are not adequate for meaningful cost comparisons.

1.5.4   Overall Observations and Recommendations

1. The heterogeneous nature of higher education is evident. Differences in the extent of machine readability and integration of data files and the appropriateness of using SCH as a measure of institutional activity are important in the handling of each type of institution. The relative success of homemade systems can be attributed to their ability to overcome the problems of heterogeneity.

2. State and federal needs for cost information are somewhat counter, at least in terms of priorities, with the needs of the institution. State interests in historical cost analyses and in programmatic categories are different from institutional interest in projection of aggregate totals and in data categorized by level and discipline.

3. Available information, current systems and the current level of administrative expertise all suggest that the process of internal management are not being given significant emphasis.

4. The current institutional view of accountability is limited. Appropriate information elements need to be defined and systems developed that address this potential need.

5. A major research effort should be undertaken to better define the decision making environment in higher education. We must know a great deal more about what decisions are being made, who is making decisions, how are decisions being made and what information is supporting the decision making processes. Further it would be helpful to have a realistically based concept of how the decision processes should operate.

6. Managerially oriented tools need to be developed. NACUBO's work with fixed and variable costing is a strong step in the right direction. A clear treatment of marginal cost with some discussion of methodology is needed.

7. Educational opportunities for administrators within institutions and for the staff personnel of state and federal agencies need to be developed.

8. External and internal information needs must be placed in juxtaposition and compared. There is an impression that exists that suggests that in large part both external and internal decision makers need the same data. Our study and analysis suggest that this impression is false. Careful analysis is needed.

9. More work should be done on categorizing institutions for different purposes. Policy issues affect different segments of higher education differently. Current categorization schemes do not adequately reflect different aspects of the institutions.

CHAPTER 2.0

DATA COLLECTION DESIGN

2.1 <u>Overall Data Collection Strategy</u>

This chapter discusses the data collection design for the research study. The data collection effort consisted of three parts; (1) site visits to 21 institutions of higher education, (2) site visits to agencies concerned with higher education in six states, and (3) a mail survey to 481 institutions. The purposes of each of these three components of the data collection effort, and their interrelationship are described in this chapter.

The purpose of the site visits to the 21 institutions was to determine how typical institutions produced and utilized cost information, and to assess the use of cost analysis methods. Since an in-depth understanding was desired, it was necessary to visit the campuses of these institutions, and to conduct interviews with a number of individuals at each site.

Because the use and production of costs was under study, only institutions were visited that had two or more years of experience with costing. Furthermore, a number of additional criteria were imposed on the site visits. As a result, it was neither possible nor desirable to select a random sample of institutions. Thus, while the results of these site visits are somewhat representative of the. experience of all institutions with cost analysis, the observations are not generalizable in a strict statistical sense.

One result of the institutional site visits was a very detailed set of case studies. The actual cases provided so much data and were of sufficient interest in their own right that it was decided to bind them into a separate volume, Monograph 3, Site Visit Descriptions of Costing Systems and Their Use in Higher Education [Schroeder, ed., 1977]. The insights gained from those cases are incorporated in Chapters 3, 4, and 5 of this volume.

The second part of the data collection effort consisted of visits to agencies associated with higher education in six states. It was decided to obtain the state perspective on demand for cost information as well as the institutional perspective, since many states require costing information. In selecting the states to be visited, only states that had been in the costing field for some time were selected. In those states selected, at least one public institution was also visited which, of course, placed a further constraint on the selection of institutions. This part of the data collection provided a state perspective on costing and specifically on the demand for cost information. It is complemented by one or more institutional views in the same state.

A mail survey to 481 institutions is the third component of the data collection effort. The purpose of this part of the data collection is to verify some of the information collected in the site visits. This sample was randomly selected and stratified to represent all higher education institutions. Thus, results of this part of the study are statistically generalizable.

The format of the mail survey was constructed roughly in parallel with the on-site survey to address issues of both the production and use of cost information. Tentative conclusions based on the site visits were primary input in the development of questions for the mail survey. But, of course, the depth of the data and the range of issues covered was much more restricted in the mail survey to keep it within a reasonable size.

Figure 1 presents a summary of the characteristics of the three different efforts. Each of these three major data collection activities is described in more detail in the following sections.

2.2 Institutional Site Visits

In our discussion of the institutional site visits below, we have presented our comments in three sections each dealing with a major aspect of the overall site visit process. These three sections cover the interview guide design, the sample selection, and the data collection itself.

2.2.1 Interview Guide Design

An extensive interview guide was developed to provide a basis for recording common data about each institution. The guide was divided into two major parts; (1) uses of cost data by administrators, and (2) production of cost data by manual or computer systems. The first part was completed by interviewing the president, chief academic officer, chief financial officer, and any other pertinent users of cost data at the institutional level. The second part was completed by interviewing those persons most familiar with costing systems (producers). In small institutions, the producers might also be the users. In larger institutions the producers were typically institutional researchers, data processing personnel or budget officers.

The users part of the survey guide was organized according to the administrative process categories discussed in detail in Monograph 1. This categorization framework has the following four major process categories.

Data Collection Component	Characteristics				
	Number In Sample	Method	Sample Selection	Questions	Result
Institutional Site Visits	21	Interviews	Judgment	Open Ended	Case Data
State Site Visits	6	Interviews	Judgment	Open Ended	Case Data
Institutional Mail Survey	481	Question-naire	Random	Mostly Closed	Statistical Data

FIGURE 1

CHARACTERISTICS OF THE DATA COLLECTION COMPONENTS

1. Resource Acquisition

2. Resource Allocation

3. Management and Control

4. Accountability

We decided to orient the interviews according to these decision processes so that something could be learned about how the process operated as well as how cost or non-cost information was used in connection with each process. This method of organization also facilitates the examination of why cost information is not used, if that is the case, and also what additional information might be desired to support the process.

In structuring the users survey guide a common series of questions was developed that applied to each of the four administrative process categories or further subcategories, if that was found to be desirable in a particular institution. The question areas for each process were: (1) how the process operates, (2) the type of information used and desired, and (3) if cost information was not used, why not? Appendix 1 is a summary version of the interview guide used with decision makers. It contains the detailed sets of questions developed for use in each of these question areas.

The producers part of the survey guide was organized by systems rather than decision processes. A system organization was selected so that one could document the life cycle of each system: (1) selection, (2) development and installation, and (3) operation. In each institution an identification was made of those primary systems that produced cost information, and each of these systems was then documented according to its life cycle.

The number of systems documented ranged from one to about three per institution. Systems documented were either (1) operational in the recent past, (2) currently operational, or (3) due to be operational in the near future. The types of systems documented can be classified as follows:

1. NCHEMS (IEP or RRPM)
2. SEARCH
3. CAMPUS
4. PLANTRAN
5. CASC Cost Study
6. Homemade Costing Systems

Each system was documented according to its life cycle. The selection phase was defined as the period from initial discussions until design and installation started. Question areas included who was involved in selection, why this particular system was selected, what the role of consultants was, etc. The design and installation phase started after selection and continued until the system reached operational status or the development was terminated. Question areas included who was involved, what problems were encountered, were they overcome, etc? The operation phase was documented in terms of system outputs, user reaction to output from the producers' perspective, and system costs. Appendix 2 is a summary version of the interview guide used with systems personnel (producers). It contains the detailed sets of questions developed for use in each of the above question areas.

The documentation of each system took two to three hours of interview time. In each case the most knowledgeable persons in the institution were interviewed.

2.2.2 <u>Sample Selection</u>

The sample for the 21 institutional site visits was selected from the population of institutions who had experience with one or more costing systems. We decided to structure this sample to meet a number of criteria rather than to select the institutions at random. The criteria chosen were as follows.

a. Include approximately four colleges from each of five "Modified Carnegie Categories."

   (1) Major research universities (Research I and II).

   (2) Private: Other doctoral granting universities and comprehensive universities and colleges.

   (3) Public: Other doctoral granting universities and comprehensive universities and colleges.

   (4) Private liberal arts colleges.

   (5) Public community colleges.

b. Represent all "cost approaches" or models

   (1) NCHEMS   (4) PLANTRAN

   (2) SEARCH   (5) CASC Cost Study

   (3) CAMPUS   (6) Mentioned in literature or by practitioners as "experienced"

c. Include only those institutions who have had two or more years of <u>experience</u> with the above costing approaches.

d. Include both institutions termed "successful" and those who have had difficulty or dropped an approach, according to the model developers. Include about 10 thought to be successful and 10 thought to have had difficulty.

e. Include some institutions in those states with developed or
    visible costing systems. States to be represented are:
    Colorado, Washington, New York, Florida, Ohio, and Michigan.

f. Include 6-10 institutions with NCHEMS experience out of the
    21 to ensure that NCHEMS experience is adequately represented.
    Also include two colleges for each of the other approaches
    listed in (b).

g. Obtain a geographic distribution in the U.S.

In attempting to meet these criteria the following selection procedure
was followed.

a. Pick supposedly "successful" colleges first to be sure to
    represent the best experience as indicated by model developers.
    Include 10-12 supposedly successful colleges spread over the
    various approaches and Carnegie classifications.

b. Pick colleges who supposedly have had "difficulty" to total 21,
    to fill out Carnegie categories, to represent states, to repre-
    sent all cost approaches, and to obtain a geographical distri-
    bution.

In picking sample institutions each model developer was contacted to
obtain recommendations on those institutions that were supposedly successful
and those institutions that had experienced difficulties. In each case a
list of institutions with two or more years of experience was available. From
the lists and discussions with developers, the sample was selected to be as
representative as possible and still meet all of the above criteria. The
resulting sample institutions are listed in Appendix 3, along with an indication of why each particular school was included in the sample.

2.2.3 Data Collection

The on-site data was collected by seven persons, each person taking
about four institutions or states for a total of 27 site visits. The interviewers consisted of four members of the project staff plus three supple-
mental persons for data collection purposes. All of these individuals were
faculty members to ensure quality data collection and proper rapport with
high level administrators.

Prior to the data collection efforts a one-day training session was
held with all seven members of the data collection team. At this session
the forms and procedures to be followed were thoroughly discussed. The data
was collected during the summer of 1975 from about September 1 to October 15.
Notes were taken on the interview guides and the interviews were tape recorded.

After each institution was visited, the interviewer completed his set
of data collection guides and wrote a summary report of the data by utilizing
the notes and tapes made during the interviews.

The on-site data summaries prepared for each institution followed the
format shown below.

    1. Uses of Cost Information
        a. Acquisition
        b. Allocation
        c. Management and Control
        d. Accountability

    2. Costing Systems
        a. System A
        b. System B
            etc.

    3. Conclusions

As noted earlier, the actual on-site case summaries are contained in Monograph 3 of this study project. Overall conclusions from the site visits were developed based on the consolidation of the conclusions in each case description, a review of the completed interview guides, and discussions involving the seven interviewers. These overall conclusions are discussed in the following chapters.

2.3 State Site Visits

The state site visits are also described below in three sections; (1) the interview guide, (2) sample selection, and (3) data collection. To reiterate, the purpose of the state surveys was to gain a state perspective on the demand for cost information, both present and future. No particular attempt was made to gain a complete understanding of state decision making processes, data collection systems or uses of cost information. Demand on institutions was the key interest in covering the state offices.

An extensive interview guide was constructed to record data collected from states. The guide was divided into the following processes:

    a.   Budgeting process - Formula

    b.   Budgeting process - Non Formula

    c.   Program Review and Approval

    d.   Private College Contracts.

For each of these processes the line of questioning included, how the process operated, the kind of cost information utilized from institutions and other sources, and the future prospects for cost information demands on institutions. Appendix 4 is a summary version of the interview guide used with state agency personnel. It contains the detailed set of questions developed for use in each of the above question areas.

Six states were selected that had extensive involvement in costing. The selection was based on the authors' knowledge, advisors' and consultants' knowledge, and literature references. States included were; Colorado, Washington, New York, Florida, Ohio and Michigan. The sample is a judgment sample of those states with extensive costing experience.

In each state all agencies were visited that had responsibility for higher education budgets or policy making. The agencies generally included a coordinating commission or board of education, an executive (governor's) budget office, and legislative staff offices. At each of these agencies from one to about six persons were interviewed depending on who had knowledge about the topics of interest.

The data was collected by the four staff members of the project during the same time period as the institutional site visits. Since all staff members had been involved in developing the state interview guide, no formal training session was needed prior to data collection.

Documentation of the interviews for the state agencies followed the same procedure as that used for the institutions. A summary was constructed and interview guides were completed utilizing tapes and notes. The conclusions from the state interviews are incorporated primarily in Chapter 6 of this volume. As noted earlier, the state cases themselves are contained in Monograph 3 of the study project.

2.4 Mail Survey

The objectives of the mail survey were:

1. to extend the investigation of institutional database characteristics, analyses of data, costing systems and

external demands for cost data undertaken in the on-site survey to a larger and randomly selected sample of institutions, and

2. to gather additional information regarding the perceptions by senior administrators of the uses and utility of cost information and costing systems and the impact of external demands for cost information.

It was desired to obtain, if possible, adequate sample data to provide a valid picture of the total population from which each institutional sample was taken with a desired degree of accuracy and confidence. Also, if possible, data were to be examined for relationships between responses to various sets of questions.

2.4.1 Definition of the Population

Because it was desired that the mail survey produce data on a sample of institutions representative of the entire spectrum of higher education, the Carnegie Classification of Institutions of Higher Education was selected as a point of departure. This comprehensive list was abridged by the elimination of professional and other specialized institutions, which were also dropped from the site visit list. This was done primarily because this group was considered too heterogeneous to produce useful data within the structure of the survey.

The quality differentiation used in the Carnegie Classification for all institutional categories except two year colleges and professional and other specialized schools was dropped from the definitional structure. Lack of precision in the application of quality definitions and the belief that use of this dimension would contribute little to the evaluation of cost analysis while greatly reducing sample cell size were the reasons for not using the quality differentiation.

A new dimension, institutional size, as measured by the number of enrolled students, was added to this modified Carnegie scheme. On this dimension each institution was placed in one of three groups: enrollment of 1000 or less, of 1001 to 3000 and greater than 3000 students. This was done in order to examine the hypothesis of other researchers that institutional size was a more critical factor determining administrative support activity than type of institution or source of control.[1] The basic Carnegie categories were retained, however, as was the identification of institutional control (public or private). Table 1 shows the resultant structure by which institutions included in the mail survey were categorized.

2.4.2 Sample Size and Selection

A list of all accredited postsecondary institutions in the United States was obtained on magnetic tape from NCHEMS. The information contained in this record included each institution's FICE code, Carnegie classification, type of control and enrollment. This information incorporated corrections of several errors in the original Carnegie designations as well as for institutions that had changed from one category to another. Project staff subsequently verified the Carnegie designations, making additional corrections as required, and updated the enrollment data to that reported in the Education Directory, 1974-75, Higher Education.

---

[1] We were influenced in this choice by Dr. Peggy Heim, Senior Research Associate, Carnegie Council on Policy Studies in Higher Education.

TABLE 1

RELATIONSHIP OF STUDY INSTITUTIONAL CLASSIFICATION
TO CARNEGIE CLASSIFICATION

Study Classification

Carnegie Classification

1. research universities

{ 1.1 research universities I
  1.2 research universities II

2. other doctoral-granting
    universities

{ 1.3 doctoral granting universities I
  1.4 doctoral granting universities II

3. comprehensive colleges &
    universities and public
    baccalaureate colleges

{ 2.1 comprehensive colleges & universities I
  2.2 comprehensive colleges & universities II
  3.1 liberal arts colleges I }
  3.2 liberal arts colleges II } public only

4. baccalaureate colleges-
    private

{ 3.1 liberal arts colleges I }
  3.2 liberal arts colleges II } private only

5. two-year institutions

4.0 two-year colleges & institutes

There were 2441 institutions recorded on the tape in the five categories selected for the study. A consideration of resource and logistic constraints indicated that the sample to be selected for the mail survey should not exceed 500 institutions. Since it was desired that a representation of the true response of all institutions in each category be obtained from the sample for that category, a small sample selection technique was employed. By this means the same level of confidence and degree of accuracy could be maintained across categories whose population ranged in size from 24 to 876 institutions.

Through use of the following technique it was determined that a confidence level of 95% with a ± .10 degree of accuracy could be achieved for all categories with an aggregate sample size of 481 institutions:[1]

$$n = [\chi^2 N(1-\pi)] - d^2(N-1) + \chi^2(1-\pi)]$$

where n = the required sample size

χ^2 = the table value of chi-square for 1 degree of freedom and desired confidence level

N = the population size

π = the population proportion which it is desired to estimate (assumed to be .50 since this would provide the maximum sample size)

d = the degree of accuracy expressed as a proportion

Table 2 gives the resultant population size for each institutional category.

Application of this small-sample technique to each institutional category size subgroup or cell (i.e., less than 1000, 1001-3000, and over 3000) revealed that an aggregate sample more than two times as large

---

[1] "Small-Sample Techniques," NEA Research Bulletin, Vol. 38, No. 4 (December 1960), pp. 99-104.

would be required to achieve the desired level of confidence and degree of accuracy for each cell. The alternative selected was to use the sample size based on the differentiation of categories and simply structure the sample for each of the five categories according to the proportion each subgroup by size is of its category. The results of this approach are reflected in Table 2.

The selection of the sample of institutions was made at the level of the individual cell or subcategory. Using the "FICE tape" obtained from NCHEMS, a computerized random number generator was used to select institutions at random within each cell until the prescribed number was obtained. The list of sample institutions printed out was then manually checked to verify the accuracy of the category designation and number of students enrolled. A second computer program was written to create a master file of the aggregated sample, listed ad seriatim by FICE code with mailing addresses and the name of the chief institutional officer. From this file address labels for all mailings were printed automatically.

2.4.3 Questionnaire Development

Development of the mail survey questionnaires was not finalized until the site visits were completed. A preliminary analysis of the site data provided a point of departure for structuring the mail survey questionnaires. Two primary thrusts for this investigation were identified: 1) the expansion of questions pertaining to cost analytic systems to obtain a more complete description of institutional databases and, 2) a focus on the perceptions of top level administrators regarding a limited number of key issues, including their impression of experience with a cost analytic system.

TABLE 2

RESPONSE RATE BY QUESTIONNAIRE, CELL, AND CELL SUBGROUP

Cell No.		Sample Size	Response Quest. I		Quest. II	
			n	%	n	%
1.1	major	0	-	-	-	-
1.2	research universities	0	-	-	-	-
1.3	-public	35	33	(94)	32	(91)
		35	33	(94)	32	(91)
1.4	major	1	0	-	0	-
1.5	research universities	1	1	(100)	1	(100)
1.6	-private	25	18	(72)	17	(68)
		27	19	(70)	18	(67)
2.1	other doctoral-	0	-	-	-	-
2.2	granting universities	0	-	-	-	-
2.3	-public	29	27	(93)	26	(90)
		29	27	(93)	26	(90)
2.4	other doctoral-	0	-	-	-	-
2.5	granting universities	2	2	(100)	2	(100)
2.6	-private	17	13	(76)	13	(76)
		19	15	(79)	15	(79)
3.1	comprehensive colleges	4	2	(50)	2	(50)
3.2	& universities-public &	21	8	(38)	3	(38)
3.3	bacc. colleges-public	50	39	(78)	38	(76)
		75	49	(65)	48	(64)
3.4	comprehensive colleges	1	0	-	0	-
3.5	& universities	29	18	(62)	17	(59)
3.6	-private	28	21	(75)	16	(57)
		58	39	(67)	33	(57)
4.1	baccalaureate	56	26	(46)	26	(46)
4.2	colleges	26	16	(62)	15	(58)
4.3	-private	1	0	-	0	-
		83	42	(51)	41	(49)
5.1	two-year	31	14	(45)	12	(39)
5.2	colleges	28	18	(64)	18	(64)
5.3	-public	27	28	(85)	22	(81)
		86	55	(64)	52	(60)
5.4	two-year	63	25	(40)	23	(37)
5.5	colleges	5	1	(20)	1	(20)
5.6	-private	1	0	-	0	-
		69	26	(38)	24	(35)
	TOTAL	481	305	(63)	289	(60)

It was presumed that the questions regarding the status of the database and analytical systems could best be answered by the person in each institution with responsibility for institutional research or data management. The nonobjective questions pertaining to the use of costing explicitly sought the response of the president, provost, chancellor or chief academic officer in each institution. Accordingly, the mail investigation was divided into two questionnaires along these lines.

Questionnaire I, "Survey of Cost-Related Academic Data and Analysis in Institutions of Higher Education," asks for the past and current database elements and the extent of integration and computerization in Part A. Part B requests information past, current and anticipated computations made with academic data. In Part C, experience with specific data and costing models, systems and concepts is identified. The workload created by external demands for cost information is the subject of Part D.

Questionnaire II, "Top Administrators' Perceptions Regarding Cost Information and Costing Systems in Higher Education," requests responses in five areas. Part A seeks perceptions of the importance of specific information for several decision processes. In Part B public institution administrators are asked to evaluate state requests for specific cost information. Part C explores the attitudes of administrators toward state and federal data requests. Attitudes regarding the usefulness of the interinstitutional exchange of cost data are sought in Part D. Part E seeks the administrator's perceptions of his institution's experience with a specific costing system. Complete copies of both questionnaires are contained in Appendix 5.

2.4.4 Logistics of the Survey

Prior to printing, each questionnaire was coded for transfer of the responses to computer punched cards. A mailing packet for each institution in the sample containing one copy each of Questionnaire I and Questionnaire II, a cover letter from Roger W. Heyns, President of the American Council on Education, addressed to the president of the institution (see Appendix 5), and two postage-paid return envelopes. Each questionnaire was identified by the responding institution's FICE number for purposes of managing the follow-up mailings.

The questionnaire packets were mailed February 5, 1976. A daily log was kept of the return rate of the completed forms. The first follow-up reminder, a postcard, was mailed to all non-responding institutions on March 5, based on observation of a significant decrease of the return rate. Reminders were also sent to institutions that had returned only one question-naire. The second and last follow-up was mailed in two stages. The first was a postcard mailed on March 17 to institutions that had returned one, but not both, questionnaires. Questionnaire packets identical to the original mailing with the addition of a reminder letter from the project director were sent to all institutions from which no response had been received on March 23. The response pattern for each of the questionnaires is shown in Figure 2. The total responses for each of the cells in the sample are shown in Table 2.

2.4.5 Preparation of the Data for Analysis

All of the returned questionnaires were edited before the data was punched onto computer cards. This consisted primarily of deleting responses that could not be used (e.g., where more than one response was given to a

Questionnaire I

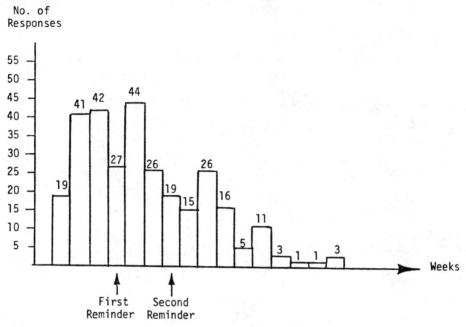

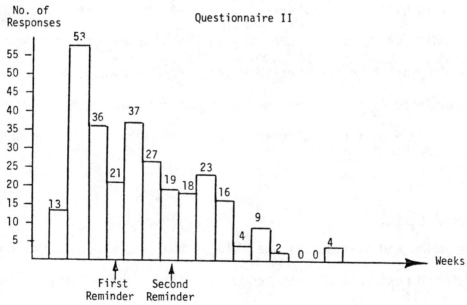

FIGURE 2

RESPONSE PATTERNS FOR QUESTIONNAIRES I AND II

question). The systems described were coded according to the following
categories:

        RRPM

        IEP

        undefined NCHEMS or RRPM + IEP

        CAMPUS

        "Homemade"

        PLANTRAN

        SEARCH

        State or college system analytical program

        Other

The edited questionnaires were then punched and verified on computer
cards. The data were entered according to the card and column schedule that
appears in gray print on the questionnaire forms. In addition, each response
set was identified by the responding institution's FICE number for card
identification and by the institutional category code for sorting and aggre-
gating the data.

2.4.6 Computer Program

Aggregation and statistical analysis of the response data was done on the
University of Minnesota's CDC 6600 computer. The aggregation program, written
in COBOL, constructed a composite database by summing the responses by question for the respondents in each cell. The punch card data was first recorded
on magnetic tape, from which the sort was made. The report generated by this
routine provided the response frequencies by question for each sample cell
(institutions by type and size).

A second program, also written in COBOL, used this composite data file to further aggregate the data and provide selected response characteristics. Reports could be generated to provide the aggregated responses for the samples of any desired set of institutional cells for any selected question or set of questions, e.g., the responses to questions 4 and 5 of Questionnaire II of all research and other doctoral granting universities. This provided, also, the ability to generate response sets for comparisons between individual cells or groups of cells. This report format also provided the weighted responses ratio for the cell population represented by the samples. To obtain the projected population responses to a given question for a single cell the following computation was made:

$$P_{a1} = \frac{N*r_{a1}}{n_1}$$

where P_{a1} is the number of institutions in the cell population that would have given answer a to question 1.

N is the number of institutions in the cell population.

r_{a1} is the number of institutions in the cell sample giving answer a to question 1.

n_1 is the number of institutions in the cell sample responding to question 1.

In order to obtain a projected population response to a given question for a group of cells the following procedure was used:

$$P_{Ga1} = \sum_{1}^{Y} P_{a1}$$

where P_{Ga1} is the number of institutions in the group of cell

populations that would have given answer a to question 1.

Y is the number of cells in the group.

P_{a1} is the population in a single cell that would have given

answer a to question 1.

CHAPTER 3.0

INSTITUTIONAL AVAILABILITY OF DATA

3.1 Introduction

Most serious discussions of institutional cost analysis usually turn to the question, what kinds of cost information do higher education institutions have and what use do they make of them? Having an appreciation for the institutional availability of cost information is important to the development of an understanding of various aspects of major costing issues. These areas of interest include: 1) an understanding of the ability of institutions in general to adopt new costing concepts and systems, 2) an estimation of the extent of change and amount of effort required for institutions to meet legislative or administrative mandates to submit cost information, and 3) development of insights into the needs and desires of institutions for costing information and building the background to understand the needs when they are expressed.

In considering the institutional availability of cost information, many different analyses are possible. There are after all many different ways to categorize institutions and many kinds of cost information to consider. Our main interest in this chapter is to provide a general picture of the status of some particular elements in the whole potential analysis that we find interesting. Thus, the results of our analysis serve as useful background to the discussions of cost systems (Chapter 4) and uses of cost information (Chapter 5). Primarily, however, the discussion below addresses specific questions or issues of interest.

Questionnaire I in Appendix 5 is the primary source of data used in this chapter although obviously some of the on-site interview data has also influenced our thinking. One of the advantages of the Questionnaire I data is that it is largely objective. Either certain data elements or file characteristics are available or they aren't. Specific data manipulations are performed or they aren't.

In the sections below we discuss the availability of some elements of basic student data, some elements of basic faculty data, and some types of computed data. Within the data computation section we review the availability of direct instructional cost data elements and a variety of special topics, such as, the availability of marginal cost data, the availability of tuition and cost comparative data, and the existence of various kinds of file integration.

3.2 Basic Student Data

Table 3 indicates the relatively high level of availability of student data that reflects activity level i.e., enrollment and student credit hour generation. The data does indicate clearly the better availability of SCH data than course enrollment data in all types of institutions except the liberal arts colleges. This probably reflects the view of the institutions that the primary measure of instructional output activity is SCH. Liberal arts colleges however are more identified with degrees and in fact many such schools do not reflect student progress in terms of credits earned but rather

TABLE 3

CURRENT AVAILABILITY OF STUDENT DATA

(% of institutions reporting the data as currently available)

Types of Student Data	Major Research	Other Doctoral	Comprehensive and 4 Year	Liberal Arts	Public 2 Year	Private 2 Year	TOTAL
Headcount by Student Level	96	100	100	100	100	100	99
FTE by Student Level	94	90	91	81	83	92	89
Headcount by Major	94	95	97	93	83	61	90
Average Course Enrollment by Discipline	88	90	91	86	78	92	87
Average Course Enrollment by Discipline and Course Level	82	73	76	76	57	70	73
SCH by Discipline	96	93	97	76	91	96	92
SCH by Discipline and Course Level	88	73	83	60	68	75	76
SCH by Discipline, Course Level, and Major	69	53	51	43	33	36	49

SOURCE: Mail Survey, Questionnaire I, Part A, Question 1 a, c, and d.

simply courses completed. The conversion from courses to credits, though relatively straightforward if desired, is just not done.

Another feature of the data is the significant drop in availability (10-20 percentage points except for the major research universities) when course level identification is added to the data element. Also, the responses of the two-year colleges is understandably weak with respect to data elements identifying activity by major.

The data identifying SCH by discipline, course level and major is the most highly specified data element in Table 3 and thus naturally the least available. This data corresponds to another question included in Questionnaire I that relates to the availability of ICLM data. For that question, responses indicate that ICLM data is available in 36 per cent of the institutions sampled and the distribution of availability by type of institution is similar to that shown for the Table 3 data. Interestingly, most of the institutions not having ICLM data indicated that its availability was a high priority in the next 2-5 year time period.

In addition to recording current availability of the various data elements, Questionnaire I also provides for the indication of the availability of data in each of the last two years, the expectation of data availability next year and whether or not having the data available in the next 2-5 year time period is a high priority. Reviewing the three year pattern of availability (current, last year, two years back) reveals no major change patterns although all types of data are becoming somewhat more available. The high priority for future development assigned to the ICLM data was noted above.

Two general characteristics of the data examined in a very cursory way were data accuracy and machine readability of the data. Table 4 indicates the relatively high accuracy rating given to student data. Surprisingly the major research universities' self-rating of the accuracy of student data is among the lowest of the types of institutions. This is probably a result of the attempts of the research institutions to make more kinds of information available, a consequent awareness of data inadequacies, and in some institutions a substantial recent enrollment growth without compensating administrative staff and system support. The machine readability of student activity data is shown in Table 5. While large proportions (77-90 per cent) of the major research, other doctoral and comprehensive institutions sampled have course enrollment and student credit hour data fully in machine readable form, Table 5 shows that significant proportions (24-50 per cent) of the liberal arts and two-year institutions sampled report that enrollment and student credit hour data files are not even partially in machine readable form. Since about 1800 institutions are in the liberal arts and two year categories we must recognize that providing computer system routines requiring use of this student data would be of little value to between 400 and 900 institutions.

3.3 Basic Faculty Data

Data related to faculty collected in Questionnaire I includes data regarding faculty assignment, salary, load, and activity. Table 6 indicates the availability of various data elements related to faculty assignment and salary. The data indicate a relatively low level of interest on the part of two-year colleges in data identifying faculty rank. Also, the disparity between the major research institutions and all the other types of institutions

TABLE 4

CURRENT ACCURACY OF DATA FILES
(% of institutions reporting good or excellent)

Types of File Data	Major Research	Other Doctoral	Comprehensive and 4 Year	Liberal Arts	Public 2 Year	Private 2 Year	TOTAL
Student Data	82	93	87	92	78	87	86
Faculty Load/ Activity Data	51	50	76	78	71	78	68
Faculty Salary Data	96	98	84	88	80	88	89

SOURCE: Mail Survey, Questionnaire I, Part A, Question 2.

sampled on the availability of average salary data by discipline is striking (94 per cent versus from 41 to 76 per cent). Apparently, research universities are more sensitive to differential salary scales by discipline than are the other institutions.

Naturally, the accuracy of the salary data as shown in Table 4 is rated relatively high. Still the fact that only 80 per cent of the public two-year colleges sampled rate the accuracy of their salary files as good or excellent is surprising. Table 5 shows the proportion of institutions where data files for faculty assignments and for faculty salaries are not machine readable as well as the proportion of institutions where this data is fully machine readable. The data indicate that the machine readability for both assignment data and salary data are similar. In total less than 45 per cent of the institutions sampled have assignment data fully machine readable while less than 50 per cent have salary data in fully machine readable form. On the other hand, about 30 per cent of all institutions sampled do not have any of their faculty assignment data or faculty salary data in even partially machine readable form. Obviously the comment noted above regarding the impact of the lack of machine readable student data is just as significant with regard to faculty data.

Availability of faculty load and activity data elements is reflected in Table 7. While credit hours is clearly the major way of expressing faculty load, the availability of contact hour load data is quite high (67 per cent of the overall sample). Two-year colleges in particular show high availability of contact hour data. As with assignment and salary data, the introduction of faculty rank as an identifier substantially reduces data availability particularly for the comprehensive, liberal arts, and two-year

TABLE 5

CURRENT MACHINE READABILITY OF DATA FILES

(% of institutions reporting files not machine readable/
% of institutions reporting files fully machine readable)

Types of File Data	Major Research	Other Doctoral	Comprehensive and 4 Year	Liberal Arts	Public 2 Year	Private 2 Year	TOTAL
Course Enrollment	2/90	0/90	6/77	34/41	26/57	48/21	15/69
Student Credit Hours	2/88	0/88	6/77	34/39	24/57	50/23	15/67
Faculty Course Assignment	15/50	10/65	27/47	44/32	43/37	52/17	30/44
Instructional Load	13/54	12/59	27/51	54/24	41/39	50/18	31/44
Faculty Activity Reports	22/34	29/29	37/25	52/5	44/22	52/5	38/22
Faculty Salaries	4/82	5/78	29/42	51/20	38/34	59/14	28/48

SOURCE: Mail Survey, Questionnaire I, Part A, Questions 3 and 4.

Table Entries: Numbers are percent of institutions reporting files not machine readable/percent of institutions reporting files fully machine readable.

TABLE 6

CURRENT AVAILABILITY OF FACULTY ASSIGNMENT AND SALARY DATA
(% of institutions reporting the data as currently available)

Types of Faculty Data	Major Research	Other Doctoral	Comprehensive and 4 Year	Liberal Arts	Public 2 Year	Private 2 Year	TOTAL
Headcount by Discipline	94	95	95	98	89	96	94
Headcount by Discipline and Rank	92	88	91	83	45	52	79
FTE by Discipline	88	88	89	83	85	85	87
FTE by Discipline and Rank	80	70	77	68	45	54	68
Average Salary by Discipline	94	76	76	76	54	41	71
Average Salary by Discipline and Rank	90	73	69	63	40	35	66

SOURCE: Mail Survey, Questionnaire I, Part A, Questions 1 e and h.

TABLE 7

CURRENT AVAILABILITY OF FACULTY LOAD AND ACTIVITY DATA
(% of institutions reporting the data as currently available)

Types of Faculty Data	Major Research	Other Doctoral	Comprehensive and 4 Year	Liberal Arts	Public 2 Year	Private 2 Year	TOTAL
Credit Hours by Discipline	88	85	97	88	78	96	89
Contact Hours by Discipline	63	61	69	50	78	76	67
Credit Hours by Discipline and Rank	59	62	51	49	28	41	49
Contact Hours by Discipline and Rank	53	55	36	32	26	39	40
Assigned Load by Discipline	51	53	83	81	72	85	71
Reported Activity by Discipline	62	64	49	34	33	53	49

SOURCE: Mail Survey, Questionnaire I, Part A, Questions 1 f and g.

institutions. The availability of faculty activity data in total is as high or higher than we expected (49 per cent of the sample) but the major research and other doctoral institutions are not as far ahead of the other types of institutions as one might expect.

The self-assessed accuracy rating of the faculty load and activity data is generally high (68 per cent of the sample indicate a good or excellent rating) especially in view of the low ratings of the research and other doctoral institutions (50 percent of the sample is good or excellent). It may be that uncertainty regarding accuracy is related to the relatively low availability of reported activity data noted above. Machine readability of faculty instructional load data (Table 5) is similar to the machine readability of faculty assignment and salary data. In comparison, however, there is an indication of somewhat less capability in the research and doctoral granting institutions and somewhat more capability in the other types of institutions.

Overall the availability, accuracy, and machine readability of faculty data seems clearly less than for student data. Nevertheless, faculty data is at reasonably high levels in all three of these areas.

3.4 Cost and Efficiency Measures

In addition to the availability of basic student and faculty data, Questionnaire I addressed the availability of some data computations related to cost and efficiency. Table 8 shows the availability of various measures relating instructional activity (SCH and FTE students) to FTE faculty. The data shown in Table 8 suggest that the availability of the activity to faculty FTE ratios is consistent with the availability of the basic student and basic faculty data. Thus, SCH by discipline per FTE faculty is the most commonly

TABLE 8

CURRENT AVAILABILITY OF AVERAGE FACULTY (PER FTE) ACTIVITY DATA
(% of institutions reporting the data as currently available)

Types of Faculty Average Data	Major Research	Other Doctoral	Comprehensive and 4 Year	Liberal Arts	Public 2 Year	Private 2 Year	TOTAL
SCH by Discipline	71	79	71	61	62	57	68
SCH by Discipline and Course Level	58	49	55	34	40	57	49
SCH by Discipline and Faculty Rank	45	37	38	25	20	19	33
FTE Students by Discipline	67	72	61	51	48	65	60
FTE Students by Discipline and Course Level	40	44	42	28	31	52	39
FTE Students by Discipline and Faculty Rank	28	37	33	21	21	15	28
FTE Students by Discipline, Faculty Rank, and Course Level	22	32	30	16	16	16	24

SOURCE: Mail Survey, Questionnaire I, Part B, Questions 1 and 2.

available measure. In general, however, the availability of all types of measures shown in Table 8 is much less than the availability of the basic student and faculty data. Still nearly 50 per cent of all the institutions sampled have data relating faculty to SCH by discipline and course level available. As with the other types of data discussed above, the additional specification of faculty rank dramatically reduces the availability of data.

Table 9 indicates the availability of direct instructional cost data. Initially, we can observe that the faculty data (per FTE) shown in Table 8 is more available than the cost data. In fact a comparison of Tables 8 and 9 indicates that many schools record the number of SCH by discipline and course level per faculty FTE but do not record the non-faculty costs that would enable them to compute the cost per SCH by discipline and course level. Also, as with the other types of data, the most commonly available form deals with SCH by discipline. It is interesting to note that discipline-related data i.e., direct instructional cost per SCH by discipline and SCH per FTE faculty by discipline has also been increasing in availability rapidly (about 10 percentage points in the last two years). Additionally, we note that the major research and other doctoral institutions show relatively low availability of data (7 to 18 per cent of the sample) on an individual course basis. Either these institutions have too many courses to manage the data problems easily or perhaps the variance among individual courses is too high to focus attention on it. Another interesting observation is that, given all the attention afforded in recent years to programmatic decision making, the availability of cost by major and cost per degree recipient seem surprisingly low (8 per cent and 17 per cent of the sample respectively).

TABLE 9

CURRENT AVAILABILITY OF DIRECT INSTRUCTIONAL COST DATA
(% of institutions reporting the data as currently available)

Types of Instructional Cost Data	Major Research	Other Doctoral	Comprehensive and 4 Year	Liberal Arts	Public 2 Year	Private 2 Year	TOTAL
Total by Discipline	78	85	71	74	71	57	73
Total by Discipline and Course Level	40	46	25	26	24	26	31
Total by Individual Course	14	15	20	21	33	29	22
Per SCH by Individual Course	18	7	20	19	20	33	19
Average per SCH by Discipline	63	70	43	45	37	33	48
Average per SCH by Discipline and Course Level	42	48	24	24	17	29	29
Average per Student Major by Student Level	22	26	18	17	10	5	17
Average per Degree Recipient by Major	6	12	10	14	4	5	8

SOURCE: Mail Survey, Questionnaire I, Part B, Question 3.

Two special questions relating to the availability of types of cost computations and two questions dealing with the availability of indirect cost allocations were also included in Questionnaire I. The availability of marginal cost data dealing with instructional programs is almost nonexistent (3 per cent of the sample). However, 37 per cent of the institutions sampled listed the availability of marginal cost data for programs as a high priority in the 2-5 year time horizon. This indicates some significant demand for the current work of the NACUBO Costing Standards Committee in the area of defining costing methodology that considers fixed and variable costs. Another special cost calculation is the comparison of tuition income to instructional cost by discipline. Questionnaire I responses indicate that 19 per cent of the institutions sampled currently have this type of data available. Proportionately more private institutions than public institutions have this data available. With respect to the allocation of indirect costs to instructional programs, 35 per cent of the institutions sampled indicate the availability of data reflecting full allocation of indirect costs.

A final somewhat technical set of questions included in Questionnaire I addressed the extent to which data files were integrated. The responses indicate that the proportion of major research, other doctoral, and comprehensive institutions having integrated data files is about twice the proportion in the liberal arts and two-year colleges. For the integration of student registration data and faculty assignment data the figures are 60 per cent to 30 per cent. For the integration of faculty assignment data and salary data the figures are 40 per cent to 20 per cent. For the ability to reclassify financial data into activity categories (crosswalk) the figures are 55 percent to 30 per cent.

3.5 Observations, Conclusions and Implications

The above discussion of the institutional availability of various types of data is necessarily brief. However, a number of interesting observations have been discussed. Some of these observations are summarized here for convenience.

- In terms of availability there is a clear ranking of types of data with student data first, faculty data second and cost data last or least available.

- The two-year colleges have a relatively low availability of student data by course level.

- A relatively large proportion of liberal arts institutions and two-year colleges have data files that are not even partially in machine readable form.

- All types of institutions have a relatively low availability of student data by major or degree.

- Other doctoral and comprehensive institutions and two-year colleges have a low availability of faculty data identified by rank.

- Faculty activity data is relatively unavailable in liberal arts and two year institutions.

- Machine readability of faculty data files is relatively uncommon particularly in liberal arts and two year institutions.

- The availability of faculty data by contact hour is relatively high particularly in two-year institutions.

- Integration of data files is a significant problem for all institutions but the level of integration is twice as high in the major research and other doctoral and comprehensive institutions as it is in the liberal arts and two year institutions.

- Availability of ICLM data is relatively low in the liberal arts and two year institutions.

- Marginal cost data is almost non-existent in all types of institutions. However, it appears to have a high priority for future development.

- The allocation of indirect costs to programs of instruction is available in relatively few institutions. However, it appears to have a high priority for future development.

These observations while certainly not conclusive have a number of potential implications.

1. Institutions (with the exception of the liberal arts group) measure their instructional activity in SCH or student contact hours by discipline. Output related measures of activity such as by major or by degree are not popular and will have to be "sold" to institutions if they are to be used.

2. Computer systems use will be impeded in many institutions because of the lack of machine readable data and the lack of file integration.

3. Development work on marginal cost techniques will be valued highly in the near future.

CHAPTER 4.0

THE PRODUCTION OF COST INFORMATION

4.1 Introduction

The purpose of this chapter is to present and analyze data regarding the systems and procedures used to produce cost information. This chapter incorporates data from both the on-site visits to twenty-one colleges and universities and the mail survey which was returned by almost three hundred institutions. A complete description of all the conditions underlying the collection of the data and the sampling procedures used was given in Chapter 2.

In this chapter, an attempt is made to summarize and highlight the important aspects of the data on systems evaluation, rather than to simply pour out the raw data. Nevertheless, the tables in this chapter contain sufficient detail so that independent analysis can be made if desired.

This chapter is organized along the same conceptual outline as that used to collect the data. The areas covered include the following:

    a. Description of the systems studied

    b. System selection

    c. Development and installation of the system

    d. System operation/evaluation

    e. Costs of systems studied

    f. Conclusions and summaries

Each of these topics is treated in a separate section below.

4.2 Systems Studied

In this section an overview of the systems studied is given. First a description is provided of the number of systems studied in depth. This is followed by a short summary of each of the available vendor systems. Finally a description of current system status is given based on the mail survey responses.

4.2.1 Systems Studied In Depth

The systems studied are classified in Table 10. The categories used in the classification recognize the function of the system (financial projection or historical cost analysis) and the source of the system (homemade or vendor supplied). In the case of financial projection systems, the classification is further specified by level of aggregation (high, medium, and low).

High aggregation is defined as aggregation at the student class level (freshman, sophomore, junior, senior and graduate) without regard to student majors, disciplines or courses. Such systems would account for costs changes due to changes in student class mix, but not due to other changes in student mix. Examples of highly aggregated systems are: SEARCH and some PLANTRAN applications that will be described later.

Medium level aggregation systems, as defined here, account for changes in student mix in terms of the number of students by major and in terms of the level of instructional activities in each discipline. Thus, enrollment forecasting and student load data must reflect not only student class, but major and discipline as well. An example of such a system is RRPM.

Finally, low aggregation systems are defined as accounting for students by major and by instructional activity to the individual course level. Such

TABLE 10

NUMBERS OF SYSTEMS STUDIED BY TYPE

Financial Projection	HOMEMADE				VENDOR SUPPLIED		
	Mail	On-site	Total	Name	Mail	On-site	Total
High Aggregation		4		SEARCH	0	1	1
Med. Aggregation	48	-	56	RRPM	26	3	29
Low Aggregation		-		CAMPUS	1	4	5
Historical Cost Analysis		4		IEP	25	5	30

OPERATIONAL STATUS OF SYSTEMS STUDIED

Financial Projection	HOMEMADE				VENDOR SUPPLIED		
	Mail	On-site	Total	Name	Mail	On-site	Total
High Aggregation		4/3		SEARCH	0/0	1/1	1/1
Med. Aggregation	48/32	-	56/39	RRPM	26/8	3/1	29/9
Low Aggregation		-		CAMPUS	1/0	4/1	5/1
Historical Cost Analysis		4/4		IEP	25/11	5/3	30/14

Table Entries: Numbers studied/numbers operational. Operational systems are those that are running in a production mode. Non-operational systems may be under development, no longer run, or may never have reached operational status.

systems allow highly refined and disaggregated analysis, as well as more aggregated analysis. The CAMPUS system is an example of a low aggregation system.

The reason for highlighting the aggregation level in this discussion is that it affects the accuracy of the system, its costs and its usefulness. Our analysis will show that the high level aggregation systems have achieved greater operational status and use than the medium and low aggregation level systems.

Table 10 shows that the systems studied were spread over all categories of vendor and homemade systems, as well as across functional purposes. It is interesting to note that we did not encounter financial projection systems with medium or low aggregation that were homemade. The homemade financial projection systems tend to be only highly aggregated. Both the high costs of constructing a disaggregated projection system and the low marginal value of such systems seem to be reasons for individual institutions avoiding their development.

Table 10 also shows the operational status of the systems studied. A simple classification is made as to whether the system was in operational status or not at the time of data collection. Operational status is defined as being run in a production mode. Non-operational status corresponded to systems that had been discontinued or have not yet reached the operational mode.

Several interesting observations emerge from Table 10. First, the low and medium aggregation systems (CAMPUS and RRPM) were usually non-operational. As we shall see later, this can probably be attributed to the cost and complexity of these systems. Secondly, the homemade systems tend to be operational. This is probably due to the evolution of homemade systems to fit the decision process and to meet management information needs. Homemade systems were constantly evolving and being modified to fit the local situation. So it appears that highly aggregated systems and/or homemade systems tend to have greater operational use than the others. We shall return to this point later.

Next, a short description is given of the common vendor supplied systems. These brief descriptions should help to orient the reader; references to more detailed descriptions of these systems are also provided.

4.2.2 Systems Descriptions

4.2.2.1 CAMPUS[1]

Several versions of the CAMPUS system have been developed (CAMPUS IX is the most recent) by SRG and SDL.[2] The CAMPUS system is a low aggregation system that can account for data down to the individual course level. As a starting point, initial enrollment input is specified by major and student level (year). Using this initial enrollment input, the system has a student flow module that projects enrollments into the future. For each year of the projection, the students are distributed (induced) to instructional activities (usually courses). The loading on courses is set by an algorithm that contains a maximum section limit. Also, CAMPUS requires as system input data the

---

[1]Comprehensive Analytic Methods for Planning in University/College Systems.

[2]SRG (Systems Research Group, Inc. of Toronto, Canada and New York) and SDL (Systems Dimensions Limited of Toronto, Canada).

courses a typical student in year x and major y is likely to take in each discipline or department. In addition, a faculty flow module is incorporated that projects the faculty levels and mix changes induced by student demand. Thus, the system requires a very complex and large database and the associated complex computer processing system. Since maximum class sizes are utilized, non-linear effects of enrollment changes can be represented. Later versions of CAMPUS incorporate program cost outputs as well as the more traditional line-item budget reports. For more information see Judy [1969] and Systems Research Group [1972].

4.2.2.2 RRPM[1]

RRPM 1.6 was developed by NCHEMS[2] as a refinement of RRPM 1.1 and the Cost Simulation Model originally developed by Weathersby [1967]. RRPM is an enrollment driven model at a medium level of aggregation. The system requires student enrollment inputs by major and year (a student flow module is separate). From these enrollment inputs, the students are distributed to disciplines and course levels by average class sizes through an induced course load matrix. This process induces a faculty teaching load on disciplines. These faculty loads in turn generate cost projections. The output is primarily in formats reflecting the NCHEMS program costing structure (PCS). The effect on costs of given enrollment inputs can be simulated for several years into the future. See Clark [1973].

---

[1]Resource Requirements Prediction Model.

[2]NCHEMS (National Center for Higher Education Management Systems) at WICHE, Boulder, Colorado.

4.2.2.3 SEARCH[1]

The SEARCH system is available from the consulting firm of Peat, Marwick and Mitchell. Since the system is proprietary, there is relatively little detailed information available on its configuration. In the one institution studied where SEARCH was installed, it was used as a highly aggregated system. Student enrollments were put in by year. This input induced a faculty load by department through student faculty ratios. Cost factors were applied to arrive at pro forma budget figures up to five years into the future. The application studied also included a revenue projection module which was unique among all of the systems observed during the study. Keane and Daniel [1970] provide a further description of the SEARCH model.

4.2.2.4 PLANTRAN[2]

This software package is supplied through MRI (Midwest Research Institute). PLANTRAN is really a computer modeling language and not a specific system like CAMPUS, RRPM or SEARCH. In the schools studied, PLANTRAN was used for highly aggregated financial planning systems, but it can be used for other types of simulation problems as well. The PLANTRAN systems were tailor made to fit each particular institution, because the PLANTRAN language only facilitates communication with the computer; it does not specify the form of the model, per se. Therefore, PLANTRAN applications are classified under homemade systems, since they are completely adapted to the particular institution. Midwest Research Institute [n.d. and 1972] contain further descriptions of PLANTRAN.

---

[1] System for Evaluating Alternative Resource Commitments in Higher Education.

[2] Planning Translator.

4.2.2.5 IEP[1]

IEP is available through NCHEMS. It is an historical costing package.
IEP does not provide future projections of cost as do CAMPUS, RRPM, or SEARCH.
IEP has been primarily designed to facilitate exchange of "comparable" information between institutions on the costs of instruction and other programs.
IEP includes several computer modules (faculty activity analysis, induced
course load matrix, etc.). The heart of IEP, however, is a crossover of
historical costs from the institution's chart of accounts to a program cost
structure. The process of using IEP begins with a reclassification of historical expenditures according to IEP definitions. Costs are distributed from
departments to standard disciplines. These costs are then associated with
majors through an induced course load matrix. The result of this calculation is the direct cost of instruction by discipline and by major. Costs
can be further allocated from supporting programs to primary programs resulting
in full costs of disciplines and majors. All of the costs are available in
a per student credit hour form to facilitate comparisons between institutions
or programs with different student loadings. Johnson and Huff [1975] and
Romney [1972] provide a more detailed description of the IEP system.

The vendor systems included in this study cover the full classification
spectrum. For financial projection systems, CAMPUS is a low level aggregation
system; RRPM is a medium level aggregation system; and SEARCH is a high level
aggregation system. IEP is an historical cost analysis system available from
vendors. PLANTRAN represents a planning language that can be used to design
your own financial projection system.

---

[1]Information Exchange Procedure.

4.2.3 Experience with Costing Systems

In the mail survey every institution was asked to describe the experience they had had with specific systems and cost concepts. The categories used in the questionnaire and the resulting data are shown in Table 11. From the table the following picture of institutional experience emerges:

1. Institutions have had greater experience with costing concepts (such as ICLM, faculty activity analysis) than with specific systems. This was expected since the concepts are more generally applicable than the systems which employ these concepts.

2. The overall operational rate for vendor systems is only forty-one out of one hundred eight systems (40%). Operational systems were those currently being run. Non-operational systems included those run in the past or those which never reached operational status. Systems still under development were not included in the one hundred eight. The operational rates by system type were (operational/total) as follows:

RRPM	17/50	SEARCH	4/12
IEP	17/27	CAMPUS	1/6
HELP/PLANTRAN	2/13	Other	22/27

These numbers from the mail survey are consistent with the on-site data already shown in Table 10.

TABLE 11

NUMBER OF INSTITUTIONS REPORTING VARIOUS TYPES OF EXPERIENCE

Specific Models/Systems		Experience					
	None	Attempted but Never Run	Run in the Past	Currently Run	Under Development	Under Serious Consideration	Would Like To Try It
NCHEMS RRPM	147	10	23	17	34	23	20
NCHEMS IEP	162	6	4	17	40	23	17
HELP/PLANTRAN	228	3	8	2	1	4	7
SEARCH	236	2	6	4		5	7
CAMPUS	231	3	2	1		4	10
Other	41	1	4	22	9	1	1
Concepts							
Induced Course Load Matrix	93	5	25	82	26	17	18
Faculty Activity Analysis	110	10	21	63	38	16	18
Enrollment Projection Modeling	109	5	16	60	33	22	27
Revenue Projection Modeling	149	4	5	44	23	20	28

SOURCE: Mail Survey, Questionnaire I, Part C, Question 1.

3. There are still a considerable number of systems under development. NCHEMS' products are taking over in this category. Very few non-NCHEMS systems were reported under development.

The picture emerges as one of limited success in systems gaining operational status, and an increasing trend toward systems supplied by NCHEMS. This will be discussed further below.

4.3 System Selection

For vendor supplied systems the selection process was relatively well defined and easy to identify. In the case of homemade systems, however, the process was difficult to identify because homemade systems tended to evolve; they were not selected during a specific period of time. Nevertheless, the issues related to selection were explored to the extent possible for both homemade and vendor supplied systems.

With regard to system selection, three main topics were explored in the study; why the system was selected, who was involved, and what alternatives were considered. These topics are discussed below.

4.3.1 Reasons for System Selection

Table 12 describes the reasons why costing systems were selected. These reasons were given by producers of cost information during the on-site visits. The reasons range from very general ones, concerning the need for better data, to specific reasons, such as, "mandated by the state." The reasons given for selecting a system are diverse. No particular reason seems to dominate. In most cases, however, there was some kind of idealism associated with the installation of a costing system. Idealism included: promoting better

TABLE 12

REASONS FOR SYSTEMS SELECTION

Incidence	Reasons
4	Need better data for internal management
1	Desire to get state out of detailed line-item budgeting
1	Need to develop a campus master plan
6	Pilot test project within a state or consortium
5	To project long-range impacts of current decisions
2	General concern with financial problems
3	Vehicle to get more state funds by showing efficiency
3	Mandated by the state
3	To obtain program-oriented data
2	Inadequate financial planning
3	Desire for comparable data

SOURCE: On-site visits to 21 institutions, Questions 16, 18 and 25 of producers interview guide. More than one reason may apply to an individual instance.

efficiency, getting better data for management purposes, and a general concern with financial pressures. Such idealism may strongly influence getting started with systems, but may not be specific enough to guide the development and installation in proper directions. A strong sense of how the system will be specifically used is also needed.

4.3.2 Influence of Inside and Outside Persons or Groups

There are three important observations regarding the influence of inside or outside groups that may be drawn from the on-site data. First, the availability of outside funding influenced the development of systems. In fifty percent of the on-site systems studied, outside funding was provided for part or all of the effort. Secondly, a strong proponent of the costing system was usually observed within the institution. Such persons were highly systems oriented either through educational background or experience. Finally, it can be observed that the state was a direct influence in costing systems selection for most of the cases in public institutions. The state exerted its influence through funding for systems, legislative mandate or state pilot projects of some type. Even for private institutions the state was sometimes an important factor, but the foundations played a greater role with respect to private institutions.

Data from the mail survey tended to reinforce and augment the above observations based on the on-site studies. Table 13 shows the mail survey data regarding the influence of inside and outside persons or groups. These questions were asked of both producers and users of cost data. From Table 13 the influence of various persons or groups on system selection ranked from high to low were as follows:

TABLE 13

INFLUENCE OF PERSONS OR GROUPS ON SYSTEMS SELECTION

		Users Response			Producers Response			Total Response		
		Yes	No	% Yes	Yes	No	% Yes	Yes	No	% Yes
a.	Influence of top administrators	78	28	73	110	77	59	188	105	64
b.	Influence of staff members members	78	24	76	83	104	44	157	128	55
c.	Request/Directive of Board of Trustees	20	59	25	24	163	13	44	222	16
d.	Requirement of a state agency	34	49	41	44	143	24	78	192	29
e.	Influence of a consultant	23	57	29	23	164	12	46	221	17
f.	Influence of a system producer	34	48	41	38	149	20	72	197	27
g.	External funding made it possible	14	63	18	18	169	10	32	232	12

SOURCE: Mail Survey, Questionnaire I, Part C, Question 2 and Questionnaire II, Part E, Question 24.

		% Indicating Yes
1.	Influence of top administrators	64
2.	Influence of staff members	55
3.	Requirement of a state agency	29
4.	Influence of a system producer	27
5.	Influence of a consultant	17
6.	Request of Board of Trustees	16
7.	External funding made it possible	12

Although the percentage of producers and users indicating these influences varied, the ranking of the influences was consistent between producers and users. One minor but interesting exception is the fact that users note the influence of the staff more frequently than the influence of themselves. Overall, internal influence of staff or administrators was the most frequently stated influence followed by the outside influences of the state, system producers, consultants and boards of directors.

4.3.3 Alternatives and Drawbacks Considered

The final issues of concern for selection were the alternatives considered and the drawbacks of the particular systems identified during the selection process. The on-site data indicates that in thirteen out of twenty-one instances, no alternatives were considered to the systems selected. In those cases where alternatives were considered, the consideration was quite cursory in about half of the instances. Thus, there were a large number of cases where the decision was essentially a go or no-go decision with respect to a particular system.

A similar situation emerged with respect to drawbacks considered. In thirteen out of eighteen of the cases no drawbacks were considered or only minor consideration of drawbacks was given. The reasons for this apparent lack of critical study were probably related to the predominance of outside funding or external requirements for systems.

It is also interesting to note that in almost all cases the systems did not replace an existing system, manual or computer. The capability being developed was entirely new, and in most cases a very significant increase in the institution's level of sophistication. There were, however, a few cases where costing systems had been evolving for ten years or more and the new systems were a natural extension of past efforts.

4.4 Development and Installation of a System

The development and installation (D & I) process starts after the system is selected or a firm decision is made to commit resources to the system and ends when the system is fully tested and run in a production or operational mode. The major questions addressed in studying the D & I process were: (1) what were the typical activities and efforts? (2) who was involved and in what way? and (3) what problems were encountered during development and installation? Each of these three questions is discussed in a separate section below.

4.4.1 Typical Activities and Efforts

For the systems studied the activities conducted during development and installation included: (1) systems design, (2) computer programming, (3) data collection and input, and (4) debugging and testing. The effort devoted to these activities is described below for each of the systems studied.

The development and installation of CAMPUS systems often extended over a period of two years. In many of the cases the CAMPUS system was not only being installed, but a new version was being developed at the same time by the vendor. For example, the efforts at the University of Colorado and the University of Toledo included development of a program costing module to interface with the existing CAMPUS software. In this case substantial systems design work was involved.

In the typical CAMPUS installation there was also a great deal of computer programming done to convert the software to the particular computer involved and to convert the institution's data files to the proper machine readable formats. For example, at the University of Colorado, the CAMPUS software provided by the vendor was extremely IBM machine dependent, and extensive programming efforts were required to convert it to Colorado's CDC equipment. Finally, a great deal of data collection and data manipulation is required for CAMPUS systems. At the University of Colorado, with considerable database problems, it took about 14 man-months to prepare the input data for the model. It took approximately nine months to get the database ready at the University of Toledo.

With regard to the RRPM and IEP systems studied, systems design and programming efforts were not nearly as great as for CAMPUS. The RRPM and IEP software is well designed from a technical point of view and not machine dependent. There was, however, usually some programming required to convert data files to the required format. Data collection and input activity required moderate to extensive efforts. For example, at Purdue, IEP data conversion took four man-months. Problems were encountered in several areas including: Purdue's fields of student and studies (majors), Purdue program centers, available faculty activity analysis, and allocation of costs. IEP data conversion at Seattle Community College required about six man-months.

PLANTRAN is a special case with regard to development and installation because PLANTRAN is really a programming language and not a system package. The institution must do its own systems design by specifying output report formats, input data, and files. The institution must also program the system utilizing the PLANTRAN language. The result is a tailor made system. Data input problems are generally minimal because the system is designed largely around the institution's existing data. Finally, the PLANTRAN systems tend to be highly aggregated and thus are extremely simple when compared to CAMPUS and RRPM. For example, at Westmar College an aggregate budget projection model was developed and installed in two months elapsed time with two man-weeks of effort.

In summary, the activities undertaken and effort expended during D & I are difficult to generalize; they depend heavily on the type of system installed, the condition of the institution's database, and the modifications desired by the institution. Estimates of time and effort are shown in Table 14 for the vendor systems studied where estimates were available. The variations in elapsed time and effort are evident.

4.4.2 Persons Involved in Development and Installation

Both inside and outside persons were involved in D & I of the systems studied. The type of inside persons involved depended on the size of the institution. In the small institutions the vice president of finance or a director of finance and budget was usually directly involved in designing these systems and even in programming them. In some cases these officers also had inside staff support, but small colleges were typically characterized by

TABLE 14

DEVELOPMENT AND INSTALLATION PHASE

Institution	System	Elapsed Time Months*	Man Months Effort On:		
			Software	Data	Total
Seattle Community College	IEP 73-74	6	0	6	6
University of Colorado	CAMPUS-Colo	12	16	14	30
University of Colorado	IEP 73-74	15+	0	12	12
Colby	CAMPUS-IX	18	N/A	4	
Westmar	PLANTRAN	2	.3	.3	.6
Purdue	IEP	6	0	4	4
Wesleyan	SEARCH	9	15	0	15
St. Petersburg	RRPM 1.6	6	N/A	N/A	N/A
Fisk	RRPM/IEP	18	N/A	N/A	N/A
University of Toledo	CAMPUS	21	12	12	24
North Dakota State School of Science	IEP	2	--	--	--

_____

*From selection of system to operational version or until abandoned.

a lack of such staff. In the large colleges and universities, the task of
D & I was frequently delegated to staff. These staff persons were often
located in an office of institutional research, or an analytic studies office,
or in data processing. The officers in the larger institutions were rarely
involved in the D & I effort after initial systems selection or design.

In the study we also noted a tendency for financial officers or institutional researchers to be more involved in these efforts than academic
officers or staff. This is particularly noteworthy since the systems typically
provide instructional costing which should affect academic decision making.
The financial management side seems to be exhibiting more interest, involvement and leadership than the academic side of the institution with regard to
costing systems. Of the twenty-two systems studied, only in three cases was the
chief academic officer or academic staff significantly involved in the systems
design effort. Two of these cases were small colleges.

In many cases there was significant involvement by outside consultants
in the D & I effort. This is quite logical since many of the systems were
vendor supplied, and the vendor had competence in particular technical details
of the system. For the systems we studied, the outside involvement by type
was as follows. CAMPUS systems had very heavy involvement by the vendor in
design and programming support. SEARCH had heavy involvement by the vendor
for a few months in the beginning. IEP/RRPM typically had only a few visits
by NCHEMS staff, unless the installation was a pilot effort or "showcase"
institution where involvement was heavy. Table 15 summarizes involvement in
these D & I efforts by outside as well as inside persons.

TABLE 15

INVOLVEMENT IN SYSTEMS D & I EFFORTS

Institution	System	Internal	External Assistance
Seattle Community College	IEP 73-74	Director of Finance and staff	Limited
University of Colorado	CAMPUS Colo.	Director of Planning and staff	Extensive
University of Colorado	IEP 73-74	I.R. and staff	Limited
Colby	CAMPUS	Department Chairman	Extensive
Westmar	PLANTRAN	Business Manager	None
Colby	L.R. Cost Projection	Administration Vice President	None
Texas Lutheran	Cost Study	Dean and I.R. Office	Limited
Purdue	IEP	Office of Analytic Studies	Limited
Purdue	Cost Study	Assistant to President, Vice President and Treasurer	None
Wesleyan	SEARCH	Treasurer and staff	Extensive
St. Petersburg	RRPM 1.6/IEP	Ed. Planning and Research	Limited
St. Petersburg	Cost Analysis System	Business Affairs	Board of Regents Staff
Fisk	RRPM/IEP	Director of Finance and Budgeting	Limited
Fisk	Financial Projection	Director of Finance and Budgeting	None
University of Michigan	Personnel Related Cost Study	Director of Academic Planning and Analysis	None
North Dakota State School of Science	IEP	Director of Computer Center	Limited
American University	PLANTRAN	I.R. staff	Limited
American University	Cost Study	I.R. staff	None
Bridgeport	CAMPUS	Manager, Computer Services	Extensive
Fullerton	RRPM	Director of I.R.	Extensive
Toledo	CAMPUS	Director of Planning	Extensive
University of West Florida	IEP	Director of I.R.	Board of Regents Staff

4.4.3 Problems Encountered

Problems encountered in development and installation will be discussed below in two parts. First, a general description of problems is given from the case data. This is followed by frequency data on problems from the mail survey.

The case data indicated a great deal of difference in problems encountered during D & I depending on the level of system aggregation. For the highly aggregated systems and PLANTRAN almost no problems were encountered. These systems, however, tended to be simple and tailor-made to the institution. The SEARCH system, at a medium level of aggregation and institution tailored, also experienced almost no D & I problems.

In contrast, the CAMPUS systems all encountered great D & I difficulties. These difficulties included programming, complexity of the model, and inadequate or erroneous data.

The IEP and RRPM systems generally encountered data problems, but little or no computer or programming problems. The data problems for IEP and RRPM included lack of account definitions, differences between institutional data definitions and system definitions, and lack of existing automated data.

In expanding the description of these problems, the mail survey included a check-off list for difficulties encountered. The data is tabulated in Table 16 and the results are highlighted as follows.

Over half of the systems encountered difficulties with data. These difficulties included database inaccuracies (53%), database not complete (53%), database not integrated (48%), and data difficult to access (35%). The next greatest difficulty encountered was in computer programming and technical

TABLE 16

DIFFICULTIES ENCOUNTERED DURING DEVELOPMENT AND INSTALLATION

	% Systems Encountering Difficulties		% Anticipated	% Overcome
	Producers	Users		
none	--	43	--	--
database inaccuracies	53	--	82	54
database not complete	53	--	77	35
database not integrated	48	--	81	42
data difficult to access	35	--	77	42
inadequate input data available	--	76	--	--
cost	31	--	61	42
computer programming	28	51	81	60
lack of technical expertise	21	34	100	38
internal opposition	27	--	86	45
insufficient funds	--	49	--	--
lack of administrative support	--	33	--	--
user resistance to using outputs	--	44	--	--

Most of the difficulties encountered were anticipated:

	strongly agree	agree	neutral	disagree	strongly disagree	don't know
Number	7	81	13	17	1	4
%	6	66	10	14	1	3

SOURCE: Questionnaire I, Part C, Question 2b and Questionnaire II, Part E, Questions 25 and 26.

expertise. Finally, insufficient funds, administrative support and user resistance were identified as difficulties.

The mail survey also included a question on whether the problems were anticipated and whether or not they were overcome. Table 16 shows that 72% of the respondents agreed or strongly agreed that most of the problems were anticipated in advance.

It is also interesting to note that about half of the data difficulties and technical difficulties were overcome, with diligence and effort. However, the problems encountered in using the information to affect decision making is quite another matter; these problems were not overcome in many cases and led to poor results, as will be discussed in the next section.

4.5 System Operation/Evaluation

System operation is used here to mean the point at which the system has reached a production mode and has begun to produce reports that are based on actual data and transmitted to users. Some of the systems studied, never reached this point. They were abandoned before the system was fully developed or during the operational testing phase prior to production of operational reports. Other systems studied were still in the development phase, during the time of the study. The focus in this section will be only on those systems which had reached operational status. Data on the numbers and types of these systems were reported in Table 10.

Three issues were studied in connection with the operation and evaluation of systems. These are: (1) distribution of systems output; (2) perceived benefits of the system output; (3) overall evaluation of the system. Each of these issues is discussed in turn below.

4.5.1 Distribution of Output Reports

The most common distribution of output reports was to the central administrative officers (president, academic officers, financial officers) and the board of trustees. In a few cases, there was no internal distribution of reports; the effort was viewed strictly as a pilot test or the reports were sent to state agencies.

Reports from the financial projection models tended to be distributed entirely to internal locations. On the other hand, reports from the historical cost analysis models were usually distributed both internally and externally. The state agencies in particular seem to have a greater concern with financial accountability through historical costing systems than with projections of financial conditions.

In a few cases the output reports stayed within the office of analytic studies, but parts of the reports were used to answer questions as they arose or for preparation of special studies. The further distillation of information by staff persons from historical or projective costing systems is an important consideration in describing these systems.

4.5.2 Perceived Benefits of Systems

The benefits picture is quite mixed. In some cases the systems produced great benefits including real impacts on decision making. In many other cases the benefits were very limited or nonexistent. A summary of the benefits identified by producers on a case-by-case basis are shown in Table 17.

The four CAMPUS systems studied produced only modest benefits. At the University of Colorado, the CAMPUS model was used to develop a master plan for the Colorado Springs campus. This plan was required by the Colorado

TABLE 17

BENEFITS OF SYSTEMS STUDIED AS PERCEIVED BY PRODUCERS CASE STUDIES

Institution	System	Benefits
Seattle Community College	IEP 73-74	Pilot test. No impact on decision making.
University of Colorado	CAMPUS	Master plan for Colorado Springs campus. Identified discrepancies in the database, superb vehicle for staff training.
University of Colorado	IEP 73-74	Pilot test only. Not fully operational.
Colby	CAMPUS	CAMPUS has not been around long enough to tell, raising consciousness of computers on campuses.
Westmar	PLANTRAN	Part of the basis for staff reallocation and reduction, developed database.
Colby	L.R. Cost Projection	More enlightened policy decisions.
Texas Lutheran	Cost Study	Raises questions among faculty about being more efficient. Affects allocation of funds to departments in a modest way.
Purdue	IEP	Raised questions about suitability of IEP for major research universities.
Purdue	Cost Study	Fulfills reporting obligations to state.
Wesleyan	SEARCH	Heart of a major financial shakedown to set priorities and place less reliance on endowment. Helped to identify serious financial situations and to arrive at corrective decisions.
St. Petersburg	RRPM 1.6	Added projection capability and program data to information systems.
St. Petersburg	Cost Analysis	To meet requirements of the state
Fisk	RRPM/IEP	Helps in determining faculty size through projection of teaching loads by department.
Fisk	Financial Projection System	Structures peoples thinking--long range impacts taken into account.
North Dakota State School of Science	IEP	Budget justification to state.
American University	PLANTRAN	Focused awareness on tuition reliance. May have helped some see interrelationships of salaries, tuition, etc. Not totally satisfactory for large institutions.
American University	Cost Study	Used for cost analysis. Too expensive to computerize. Switching to IEP.
Bridgeport	CAMPUS	Use of ICLM data. Used to set tuition rates for part time and full time students.
Fullerton	RRPM	Better database. Some use of ICLM. Full disclosure of all data to all administrators. Not compatible with decision process.
Toledo	CAMPUS	Exposed weaknesses in data and computer staff.
University of West Florida	IEP	Mandated by state. Used to develop new state allocation formula.
University of Michigan	Personnel Related Case Study	Source of data needed in the budget process and to meet state requests.

Commission on Higher Education. An attempt was also made to use the CAMPUS

system on the Boulder campus for policy and operational decision making on

that campus. This effort was not successful. At Colby College, CAMPUS has

not provided tangible benefits although more than a year has passed since it

reached operational status. The intangible benefits at Colby include a greater

consciousness of computerization on campus and improvement of the database.

The SEARCH model has greatly affected decision making at Wesleyan College.

The model helped identify serious financial problems including the need for

cutbacks and less reliance on endowment. According to administrators at

Wesleyan, the future erosion of endowment funds was not clear until model

projections were made. The SEARCH system has also helped in evaluating the

impact of alternative plans for cutbacks and financial belt tightening.

PLANTRAN and the highly aggregated financial projection models have pro-

vided moderate institutional benefits including information for staff reallo-

cations, more enlightened decision making, and an ability to project future

consequences of decisions. Since these models are tailor-made and relatively

simple, they tend to be a part of the annual budget and planning cycle.

Generally speaking, these models provide structure to data and they help

quantify administrators' intuitions concerning financial decisions.

The historical cost analysis and IEP systems have been found to have

little impact on internal institutional decision making. In some cases it was

too early to tell what the ultimate impact might be. However, the historical

costing systems usually were designed for outside accountability purposes.

They often fulfilled reporting obligations to the state.

The mail survey also resulted in data concerning systems benefits. This data was collected from users and is tabulated in Table 18. The following implications are drawn from this data.

Administrators' perceived benefits do vary by system and the various potential uses for the system outputs. From thirteen to eighty-nine percent of the administrators found the various types of benefits to be worthwhile. The highest benefit levels are associated more with the long range and external issues than the issues of day-to-day institutional management.

By model type, the homemade models showed a significantly higher perceived benefit in several categories than the vendor supplied systems. Only in the category of data supplied to outside agencies did the perceived benefit of a vendor supplied system (IEP) exceed the homemade systems. On the other hand, the percent of administrators who perceived a benefit of homemade systems for day-to-day institutional management exceeded the vendor systems by over two to one. So the homemade systems appear to be much more worthwhile for internal use than vendor systems, while the reverse is true for external use.

4.5.3 Overall Evaluation and Expectations

An attempt was made in the cases involving site visits to determine whether the system met the expectations of various individuals, and if it did not, why not? The highly aggregated models, which were the most successful, also tended to meet expectations to a high degree. Low aggregation systems for financial projections were more complicated and often fell short of expectations in terms of their impact on decisions. These low aggregation systems also generally required more hand input of data than expected and resulted in more programming than the producers expected in advance.

TABLE 18

BENEFITS OF SYSTEMS AS PERCEIVED BY ADMINISTRATORS

	Benefit	Percent Indicating Benefit				
		Homemade	RRPM	IEP	Other Systems*	All Systems
a.	day-to-day insti-tutional management	58	31	13	39	40
b.	long range planning	86	67	47	77	73
c.	better interpretation of institutional data	82	67	81	83	79
d.	better data for external inquiries	69	46	73	72	65
e.	better information for allocation of resources	89	50	53	70	70
f.	forecasting	74	48	33	64	60
	Number of Systems Reported	50	28	25	33	136

*Included 1 CAMPUS, 1 PLANTRAN, 10 NCHEMS, 8 State Mandated and 13 Unidentified.

SOURCE: Mail Survey, Questionnaire II, Part E, Question 29.

Regarding overall evaluation, the producers generally felt that the systems provided some useful benefits. In some cases, the systems were acknowledged to be technical successes, but had little impact on the decision process. Nevertheless, the producers were positive about the benefits. When asked whether the level of benefits were adequate for the costs, most producers responded in the affirmative.

A more detailed evaluation of specific systems was provided by users as part of the mail survey. Several questions addressing the overall evaluation of the benefits of a specific system used at the respondents institution were included. In Table 19, responses to these questions are tabulated. These responses show that:

1. Seventy-nine out of 120 administrators (66%) agreed or strongly agreed that the systems studied had produced useful information for decision making within their institutions. This agreement was strongest for homemade systems (80%) and weaker for RRPM (43%) and IEP (50%) systems.

2. When asked whether the system would eventually produce useful information, 84 percent agreed or strongly agreed. The percentages by type of system were: homemade (88%), RRPM (70%), and IEP (89%).

3. Seventy-three out of 122 administrators (60%) agreed or strongly agreed that the benefits had outweighed the costs of the system. Percentages by type of system were: homemade (69%), RRPM (52%) and IEP (47%).

TABLE 19: USER EVALUATION SYSTEMS

	Number of Responses						
System	strongly agree	agree	neutral	disagree	strongly disagree	don't know	total
	This system has produced useful information for decision making within your institution.						
RRPM	0	12	6	7	2	1	28
IEP	2	7	3	4	0	2	18
Homemade	9	26	6	2	1	0	44
Others	3	20	2	4	1	0	30
All	14	65	17	17	4	3	120
	This system will eventually produce useful information for decision making within your institution.						
RRPM	4	15	3	3	1	1	27
IEP	4	13	1	0	0	1	19
Homemade	10	25	3	1	1	0	40
Others	7	19	0	4	0	0	30
All	25	72	7	8	2	2	116
	The benefits to your institution have outweighed the costs of this system.						
RRPM	0	14	3	6	1	3	27
IEP	3	6	3	4	0	3	19
Homemade	10	21	7	2	1	4	45
Others	4	15	5	6	0	1	31
All	17	56	18	18	2	11	122
	A greater involvement on the part of administrators would have been beneficial in the selection and design of this costing system.						
RRPM	3	9	7	6	2	1	27
IEP	2	3	6	6	-	2	19
Homemade	4	13	16	9	1	1	44
Others	6	11	7	6	0	1	31
All	16	36	35	27	3	5	121

SOURCE: Mail Survey, Questionnaire II, Part E, Questions 27, 28, 30, and 31.

These evaluations lead to several conclusions. First, for internal uses homemade systems consistently obtain higher overall evaluations than vendor provided systems. Secondly, only about half of the users agree (or strongly agree) that their experiences with RRPM and IEP have been beneficial or that the benefits have outweighed the costs. Most of these users are however optimistic that the systems will eventually produce benefits to the institution.

In an attempt to partially explain the reasons for these results a question was included that asked whether a greater involvement on the part of administrators would have been beneficial in the solution and design of their costing system. Forty-two per cent agreed or strongly agreed, 29% were neutral and 29% disagreed or strongly disagreed. This indicates that some additional involvement by administrators may tend to improve the usefulness and benefits of these systems. However, the question about how to improve modeling effectiveness is indeed complicated and was not explored in great depth in this study.

4.6 System Costs

An effort was made in the on-site visits to determine the costs of the systems installed. In many institutions reliable records or even educated guesses were not available. Out of the twenty-two systems studied, we were able to collect usable data on fourteen of them. These costs are shown in Table 20.

In tabulating the cost data, the development and installation cost is separated from the annual cost of system operation. Before collecting these numbers, definitions were developed for each category in detail (see Appendix 2). Generally speaking D & I cost includes all costs incurred until the system

TABLE 20

ESTIMATED COSTS OF SYSTEMS

College	System	Development and Installation	Annual Operation	Runs/Year
North Dakota State School of Science	IEP	$ 1,085	$ 1,950	3
Fisk University	Financial Projection	1,250	325	30
Fisk University	PPBS	1,300	3,200	1
St. Petersburg Junior College	Cost Analysis	14,370	15,700	2
St. Petersburg Junior College	RRPM	6,400	850	6
University of Colorado	CAMPUS	110,500	------	--
University of Colorado	IEP	35,000	30,000	
Seattle Community College	IEP	12,777	N/A	N/A
Wesleyan University	SEARCH	68,000	850	100
Purdue University	IEP	15,000	22,400	
Purdue University	Cost Study	21,700	7,100	2
Purdue University	Direct Cost Study	7,300	7,600	2
University of Toledo	CAMPUS	120,000	------	--
University of Michigan	Personnel Related Cost Study	180,000	100,000	1

reached production status including systems design, programming, clerical support, computer time, supervision and initial database preparation. The annual operating costs included; program maintenance, computer operations, and data input costs.

The D & I costs range from a low of $1,085 to a high of $180,000. On the low end the costs generally included only installation of available vendor programs and the use of existing databases. On the high end, the costs usually involved a complete development from scratch or a very substantial modification to vendor programs together with extensive work on data input. The existing condition of the institution's database seems to be an important factor in affecting D & I costs along with the amount of design and programming needed.

The operating costs varied from a low of $325 a year to $100,000 a year. The low end of these costs referred to very simple models, and the high end to major universities with large data inputs and complex systems.

Since the costs vary so much by type of system and type of school, it is not possible to seek general conclusions from this data. It is, however, important to recognize the large sums which can be involved and to carefully estimate the "real" costs of systems prior to installation.

The costing efforts made in this study represent a first step in attempting to understand the costs of costing systems in higher education. Clearly, research in this area needs to be initiated.

4.7 Observations, Conclusions and Implications

Systems were selected for many different reasons including better data, concern with financial problems, state influence, and a desire for improved long range planning. In many cases, however, institutions viewed these systems development efforts as pilot tests rather than operational decision making support efforts. Thus perceptions of benefits should be viewed with this intent in mind. The surveys indicated that administrators, staff, states and funding agencies all played roles in system selection. No single type of person or group seemed to dominate the selection process.

The activities and problems encountered during system development and installation depended on the type of system. The less aggregated systems (CAMPUS and RRPM) seemed to take longer to install and encountered more difficulties than the highly aggregated systems. In cases where outside vendors were involved the greatest difficulty encountered was in developing the necessary input data. Homemade systems encountered much less difficulty in this regard because they were largely fitted to existing institutional databases. After data problems, the most frequent difficulties encountered were computer programming and lack of technical expertise followed by poor administrative support and user resistance. Almost all systems efforts encountered some of these problems. It was the rare case that went without a hitch.

The development and installation effort was generally handled by staff except in small institutions where the line officers were also the staff. With the CAMPUS model, the vendor was usually heavily involved in D & I. For IEP and RRPM, the vendor provided limited services acting in most cases as the supplier. Academic officers had a disproportionately small influence on systems development compared to financial officers and their staffs.

The distribution of output reports for these models exhibited an interesting pattern. While reports for financial projection models were usually limited to internal distribution, reports from historical cost systems were distributed both internally and externally. This distribution pattern reflects the greater interest of states in accountability through historical costing, while institutions are more interested in projecting their future financial condition.

In general the benefits picture for systems that produce cost information is mixed. While some institutions perceive a great benefit, others perceive no tangible benefit. CAMPUS systems generally produced little or no impact on institutional decision making. Many CAMPUS systems are no longer running after the initial trial period because they proved to be too complex and costly to install and use. In the one application of SEARCH studied in depth, the model was highly aggregated and successfully used to project financial conditions. The model was supported by a high level of internal expertise and a "felt need" on the part of the college. IEP has had little impact on internal decision making in the institutions studied, but was seen as beneficial for external purposes. IEP has in most cases helped raise the institution's accountability image, and fulfilled reporting obligations.

From the mail survey it was found that homemade systems had significantly greater perceived benefits than vendor supplied systems for internal decision making. Institutions also encountered less problems in making homemade systems operational.

Only about half of the users agree or strongly agree that their experiences with IEP or RRPM have been beneficial for institutional decision making and that the benefits have outweighed the costs. However, these users are optimistic that IEP and RRPM systems will eventually produce benefits for the institution.

In summary, the study seems to substantiate the following points:

1. Homemade systems provide greater perceived benefits than vendor supplied systems for internal decision making.

2. In only about half of the cases, administrators felt that RRPM or IEP systems have provided useful information. In the other half of the cases these systems were viewed as pilot tests or they never reached useful operational status.

3. For financial projections highly aggregated systems such as PLANTRAN and SEARCH tended to be much more useful than the more disaggregated RRPM and CAMPUS systems.

4. Cost projection systems are of greater use for internal financial planning, while historical costing systems are better suited to accountability concerns.

Based on our review of the data we have collected, the following implications and recommendations are offered for institutions:

1. Institutions should identify in advance specific needs and uses for systems in addition to general needs such as better data and better planning. These specific uses will help guide selection and development of the system and enhance operational use after the system is installed.

2. Academic officers and other users should become more involved in system design. Such involvement is likely to lead to a better understanding of the model by the users and informed use of the model.

3. Institutions should consider highly aggregated cost projection systems. These systems should project total revenues and expenditures on an aggregate level. If more detail and accuracy is needed, these projection models can be refined to include more disaggregation. In other words, cost projection models should be built from the top down and expanded in an evolutionary fashion as needed.

4. Greater attention should be paid to defining the type of system needed and its uses prior to system development. The study showed very little consideration of alternative systems by many institutions.

5. For historical costing or large financial projection systems, an institution should be prepared to devote considerable effort in improving input data and in installing the system on the computer. The data conversion and programming efforts should be carefully estimated in advance. The amount of effort required will vary greatly with the type of system selected and the condition of institutional database, computer expertise, etc.

6. Administrators should recognize that it is very difficult (and perhaps impossible) in most cases to meet external needs and internal needs for data from the same system. The systems studied tended to primarily emphasize their external needs or internal needs, but not both.

7. Homemade systems should be considered for _internal_ decision making. These systems tend to achieve a greater degree of use than externally supplied systems, because homemade systems

do a better job of meeting institutional needs. Vendor systems should only be considered after needs are carefully identified.

8. Vendors and institutional staff should consider providing modeling services as well as supplying models. These services should concentrate on identifying information needs, user education, and analysis of model outputs. Such efforts will view service and better decisions as the product rather than the model as the ultimate product.

9. Efforts should concentrate on concept installation as well as model installation. Concept installation involves changing decision processes and decision making styles. Such changes in concepts are often required before informed use of a model can take place.

10. Institutions should consider a staged plan to improve the use of cost information. It is perhaps too much to expect both concept and model installation to occur at once. A more evolutionary approach toward change is warranted.

CHAPTER 5.0

INSTITUTIONAL USE OF COST INFORMATION

5.1 Introduction

In Chapters 3 and 4 we discussed the institutional availability of cost and cost related data and the production of cost information. This chapter will review our observations regarding the use of cost information and cost analysis in academic institutions. The research project's first monograph, "The Literature of Cost and Cost Analysis in Higher Education," described a framework for discussion that was directly related to the use of costing information. We called that categorization the administrative processes framework. Its major categories included: resource acquisition, resource allocation, resource management and control, and accountability. It seems appropriate to us to use this same structure in reporting on the data we have gathered about the use of cost information. Thus we have structured this chapter to include a section on each of the four major administrative processes categories.

In addition to the sections corresponding to the administrative processes categories, we have chosen two special topics to discuss in separate sections. These two topics, state/federal mandated information and exchange of data are included because of their special interest and importance. One of the initial motivating factors behind our entire study was the concern over the possibility of federally mandated submission of instructional unit cost data.

The two primary sources of data which are the basis of our discussions in this chapter are the on-site interviews with twenty-one colleges and universities and the mail survey of 481 institutions. Where the responses for either of the types of data vary significantly by type of institution we indicate this in the tables and the discussion. These variations are in terms of categories of size of the institutions (large, medium, small), type of institutional control (public, private), and the programmatic types of institutions (major research, other doctoral granting, comprehensive, baccalaureate, and two-year). In some cases these variations are large and may have implications for policies adopted by government agencies. Where no variation is shown in the tables of this chapter, that indicates no significant variation from the overall average response of all types of institutions.

Table 21 provides an overview of the different ways in which institutions use instructional unit cost data. The response rate to this question was nearly 50 per cent. Significantly 13 per cent of the respondents indicated no direct use of unit cost data. Among the types of uses noted, by far the largest usage is to spot problem areas (95 per cent of those indicating use included this usage). We assume that problem identification occurs mainly in the area of allocation and control activities and is related to the allocation decision use (72 per cent indicate usage) and the increase confidence use (83 per cent indicate usage). The uses of justifying decisions (58 per cent usage), dealing with criticisms (72 per cent usage) and providing a good image (49 per cent usage) are more related to accountability and to some extent resource acquisition. These uses are clearly less common to all institutions than those dealing with allocation and control.

TABLE 21

USES OF INSTRUCTIONAL UNIT COST DATA

Type of Use	Percentage of All Types of Institutions Indicating Usage* (Approximately 50% Response Rate)
Allocation Decisions	71
Justify Decisions	58
Spot Problem Areas	95
Increase Confidence in Decision Making	83
Deal with Criticisms	72
Provide Image of Good Management	49

---
*Percentages shown are of those responding to each type of use; 13 per cent indicated no direct use of unit cost data.

SOURCE: Mail Survey, Questionnaire II, Part A, Question 6.

5.2 Acquisition of Funds

Administrative processes in this category include tuition setting, estimation and justification of resource requirements, and cost recovery rate setting. Most of our discussion will deal with the area of estimating and justifying resource requirements. On the basis of our site visits, the cost recovery rate setting process is viewed simply as an accounting or auditing process. Virtually no cost analysis comes into play in deciding cost recovery rates. It is conceivable that careful cost analysis would result in differential cost recovery rates for different types of research and service projects or in an institutional preference for certain kinds of research or service projects. However, the process is generally viewed as one of simply following government rules or using accepted accounting practices.

Tuition setting is another process in which cost information and analysis seems to play a very minor role. Except for one institution (University of Bridgeport), the on-site data suggests that either tuition rates are legislated or the decision is based on balancing the revenues and expenditures with some consideration of the rates set by comparable schools. In general no cost analysis comes into play. With the one exception (Bridgeport), no attempts to base differential tuition on cost analysis were observed.

The process of estimating and justifying resource requirements is more closely related to cost analysis. As noted in our first monongraph, the distinction between acquisition and allocation as they relate to estimating requirements is clearer in a public institution than in a private one. In public institutions the estimation process is the primary interaction with external sources of support.

Unless the enrollment is stabilized, as it is, for example, at the University of Michigan, the University of Colorado, and the University of Wisconsin at La Crosse, enrollment forecasting is the key data analysis activity. Costs are relatively insignificant by comparison. The orientation of the state organization is also important. States with a strong executive or coordinating group seem to favor some form of formula support, whereas, states with strong legislative influence seem to prefer a line item by institution approach. The latter approach of course allows for more preferential treatment of particular institutions.

Use of formulas for determining subsidy or support levels requires some form of comparative cost analysis to justify the formula. Because of the importance of data exchange we are discussing that subject as a separate section. This discussion is not duplicated here. However, the attitudes of the public institutions to various aspects of formula support are interesting. Table 22 indicates that only 50 per cent of the institutions agree or strongly agree that instructional unit costs can be useful for developing support formulas. The one category of institutions that exhibited significantly stronger agreement than the others was the other doctoral and comprehensive institutions (67 per cent). As will be seen in our discussion of data exchange, a good part of the lack of agreement that unit costs can be useful in formula development may be the result of a perception that technical problems with current data analysis techniques cannot be overcome.

In addition to the problems with instructional unit costs, the use of formulas in computing state support also raises other issues. As shown in Table 22, 71 per cent of the institutions feel that use of formulas increases

TABLE 22

ATTITUDES TOWARDS STATE FORMULA SUPPORT

	Per Cent (Public Institutions) Agree/ Strongly Agree	Per Cent (Public Institutions) Disagree/ Strongly Disagree
Instructional Unit Costs Can Be Useful for Developing Support Formulas		
All Types of Institutions	50	28
Other Doctoral and Comprehensive Institutions	67	27
Use of Formulas Decreases Level of Effort for Budget Submission		
All Types of Institutions	32	53
Major Research Institutions	15	49
Other Doctoral and Comprehensive Institutions	40	51
Baccalaureate Institutions	33	33
Two-year Colleges	31	56
Use of Formulas Increases the Threat of State Control		
All Types of Institutions	71	17
Use of Formulas Allows More Time for Internal Management		
All Types of Institutions	25	56
Use of Formulas Makes Planning Easier and More Certain		
All Types of Institutions	37	41
Major Research Institutions	28	47
Other Doctoral and Comprehensive Institutions	46	36
Baccalaureate Institutions	33	33
Two-year Colleges	31	44
Use of Formulas Tends to Direct Internal Allocation		
All Types of Institutions	52	38
Large Institutions	49	33
Medium Size Institutions	56	17
Small Institutions	65	12

SOURCE: Mail Survey, Questionnaire II, Part B, Questions 10 and 11.

the threat of state control of the institution. Also, 52 per cent believe that the use of support formulas tends to direct internal allocations. One of the universities visited had a recurring problem with one of its schools because internal allocations were not consistent with state support levels. Three types of possible advantages were also considered and they received a less than enthusiastic response as shown in Table 22. Only 32 per cent of the institutions agreed or strongly agreed that the use of formulas to determine support reduced the effort required for their budget request submission. The figure for major research institutions was only 15 per cent. Also, only 25 per cent of the institutions agreed or strongly agreed that the use of formulas for determining support allowed more time for internal management. However, 37 per cent of the institutions did agree or strongly agree that the use of formulas to determine support made planning easier and more certain.

5.3 Allocation of Available Resources

For most academic institutions the allocation of resources is the primary or most important administrative process. Budgets, which document the allocation decisions, are not only the authority for undertaking various activities but frequently they are a principal source of communication regarding plans, policies and priorities in the institution. Perhaps because the allocation process is so central and important, a relatively extensive array of cost information and cost analysis has been associated with it. Later in this section we will examine the perceived usefulness of different types of cost information in the allocation decision process. Before doing that, however, it is important to consider the role of cost information in the allocation decision process in a more general way.

Based on the observations made during the on-site visits we would con-
clude that cost is not a dominant consideration in most allocation decisions.
In fact, in many allocation decisions cost is not even very important. Issues
of program completeness, program quality, institutional priorities and interpersonal relations frequently outweigh the impact of cost considerations on allocation decisions. One factor that is generally important in allocation decisions
is load. For many institutions the level of resources and mix of program
offerings is relatively fixed and allocation is really reallocation. In such
cases changes in load, whether it is instructional or service support load, are
important considerations. One special allocation case is the decision to
initiate new programs. While administrators are interested in the cost of new
programs at an aggregate level, the "bottom line" so to speak, they generally
do not consider cost analysis as very important. An officer of one of the large
universities visited said in effect that if you tell a department or college
that you can't afford a new program that is being proposed they will be back
the next day with a proposal to conduct the program at zero marginal cost.
Most of the analysis supporting new program proposals is done on an ad hoc
basis. As a result, the cost figures in particular are uncertain and the
value and attractiveness of the program seem to be overriding.

The on-site visits also pointed out that managerial style at an institution is an important determinant of the role of cost analysis. If the
style is political and participative, cost information and analysis tends to
be less important. On the other hand, if the style is rational and authori-
tarian, cost information and analysis tends to be more important. While we
have noted that cost information and analysis is not always a dominating
consideration in allocation decisions, it is important. In the remainder of

this section we review the use of cost and cost related data in the allocation process.

Cost related data is data about factors in the instructional process that determine or at least imply costs. Examples are: class size, faculty workload, student/faculty ratios, and faculty salary rate. A unit with a small average class size is likely to be a high cost unit and a unit with high student/faculty ratios is likely to be a low cost unit. Table 23 displays the percentage of institutions that rate as important or very important various cost related data in the allocation decision process. The lower importance attached to the factors shown in the table by small schools and private schools is consistent with the relatively low availability of such data reported in Chapter 3. As shown in Table 23, faculty workload is given the highest level of importance (88 per cent rate it as important or very important) and student/faculty ratio data is also rated high (82 per cent rate it as important or very important). The high rating of this data indicates an interest in equity for individual faculty members. For student credit hours produced, 84 per cent of the responses indicated a rating of important or very important. This reinforces our earlier comments about the concern for load in making allocation decisions. The difference in the public institution response (94 per cent) and the private institution response (72 per cent) regarding the importance of student credit hours produced reflects the different outlooks of the two types of institutions about how their activity or output should be viewed. Average class size is rated important or very important by 78 per cent of the respondents. This goes along somewhat with the faculty workload and student/faculty ratio data. Faculty salary rate is undoubtedly a major determinant of instructional costs but in Table 23 it

TABLE 23

IMPORTANCE OF VARIOUS TYPES OF NON-COST DATA IN GOVERNING ALLOCATIONS

Types of Data	Percentage of Institutions Rating Information as Important or Very Important
• Average Class Size	
All Types of Institutions	78
Public Institutions	82
Private Institutions	73
Two-year Colleges	86
• Faculty Work Load	
All Types of Institutions	88
Large Institutions	89
Medium Size Institutions	92
Small Institutions	73
• Student/Faculty Ratios	
All Types of Institutions	82
Public Institutions	87
Private Institutions	78
Medium Size Institutions	87
Small Institutions	77
• Faculty Salary Rate	
All Types of Institutions	59
Major Research Institutions	61
Other Doctoral and Comprehensive Institutions	52
Baccalaureate Institutions	63
Two-year Colleges	66
• Student Credit Hours Produced	
All Types of Institutions	84
Public Institutions	94
Private Institutions	72
Large Institutions	88
Medium Size Institutions	83
Small Institutions	75
Major Research Institutions	86
Other Doctoral and Comprehensive Institutions	87
Baccalaureate Institutions	70
Two-year Colleges	86

SOURCE: Mail Survey, Questionnaire II, Part A, Question 1

receives the lowest rating (59 per cent rate it as important or very important) of importance. This may be because the salary rates for different disciplines, departments or units are expected to be different so that data presenting these differences is not highly valued. On the other hand, the salary rate structure may be viewed as controlled by general market forces and therefore not really an allocation decision. Differences are thus interesting but unimportant.

Another type of data that is like cost related data is the data reflecting credit hours taken in each discipline by students in each major. This data is referred to as induced course load matrix (ICLM) data. Table 25 shows that 38 per cent of the respondents agreed with the statement that ICLM data are useful in the allocation of instructional funds while 28 per cent disagreed. This ambivalence to ICLM data is difficult to explain but it is consistent with the low availability of ICLM data reported in Chapter 3. Perhaps it is a further indication of the relative lack of interest in data related to degrees and majors noted in the earlier discussions of data availability.

The ratings of the importance of unit cost data are definitely lower than the ratings of the importance of cost related data. Table 24 shows that the proportion of institutions in our sample that rate cost per SCH by discipline as important or very important in the allocation process is 56 per cent. There is some variation in this response by type of institution. For major research institutions, the percentage is only 46 and for two-year colleges it is 60 per cent. The importance of the cost per SCH by department is somewhat higher. Table 24 also shows that 66 per cent of the institutions in our sample rated the cost per SCH by department as important or very important.

The importance of data related to output or activities measured in terms of degrees or majors is rated considerably lower than the cost data related

TABLE 24

IMPORTANCE OF VARIOUS TYPES OF UNIT COST DATA IN GOVERNING ALLOCATIONS

Types of Data	Percentage of Institutions Rating Information as Important or Very Important
• Cost Per SCH by Discipline	
All Types of Institutions	56
Major Research Institutions	46
Two-year Colleges	60
• Cost Per SCH by Department	
All Types of Institutions	66
Public Institutions	71
Private Institutions	59
Small Institutions	54
Major Research Institutions	71
Baccalaureate Institutions	57
• Cost Per Degree Granted	
All Types of Institutions	23
Major Research Institutions	17
Other Doctoral and Comprehensive Institutions	25
Baccalaureate Institutions	32
Two-year Colleges	30
• Annual Cost Per Student by Major	
All Types of Institutions	36
Major Research Institutions	29
Other Doctoral and Comprehensive Institutions	31
Baccalaureate Institutions	51
Two-year Colleges	39
Large Institutions	32
Medium Size Institutions	40
Small Institutions	39

SOURCE: Mail Survey, Questionnaire II, Part A, Question 2.

to the activities of disciplines and departments. Table 24 shows that only 36 per cent of the institution in our sample rated annual cost per student by major as important or very important in the allocation process. An interesting exception to the low overall rating level is the baccalaureate institutions with a 51 per cent rating. As Table 24 also shows, the proportion indicating that the cost per degree granted is important or very important is only 23 per cent. At present it would appear that allocation decisions are made in terms of a decision structure that is related to disciplines and departments rather than to instructional programs. This of course is consistent with the lack of availability of program data indicated in Chapter 3.

Since there appears to be a difference between the relative importance of unit cost data and cost related data as well as other forms of cost data, some direct comparison questions were included in the mail survey. Table 25 shows the response of the institutions in the sample to a statement that total costs and cost ratios (proportions) were more important than unit costs in the allocation of instructional funds. For all types of institutions 49 per cent agree or strongly agree that cost related data is more important while 31 per cent disagree or strongly disagree. Major research institutions favor total costs and ratios more than the overall average (with a 55 per cent agree/24 per cent disagree response) while other doctoral and comprehensive institutions favor total costs and ratios less than the overall average (with a 44 per cent agree/36 per cent disagree response).

In response to the direct comparative statement that process factor data, such as class size and student/faculty ratios are more important than unit cost data in the allocation of instructional funds, 68 per cent of the

TABLE 25

RELATIVE IMPORTANCE OF VARIOUS TYPES OF COST AND NON-COST DATA IN ALLOCATION DECISIONS

	Per Cent Agree/ Strongly Agree	Per Cent Disagree/ Strongly Disagree
Total Costs of Instruction and Cost Ratios Are More Important In the Allocation of Instructional Funds Than Unit Cost Data		
All Types of Institutions	49	31
Public Institutions	52	31
Private Institutions	44	32
Major Research Institutions	55	24
Other Doctoral and Comprehensive Institutions	44	36
Baccalaureate Institutions	45	37
Two-year Colleges	54	27
Instructional Process Factors are More Important In the Allocation of Instructional Funds Than Unit Cost Data		
All Types of Institutions	68	12
ICLM Data Are Useful In the Allocation of Instructional Funds		
All Types of Institutions	38	28
Baccalaureate Institutions	24	24

SOURCE: Mail Survey, Questionnaire II, Part A, Questions 4, 5, and 7.

institutions responding indicate agreement or strong agreement while 12 per cent disagreed or strongly disagreed. An open-ended question was also included in Questionnaire II that asked for comments on the relative usefulness of instructional process data versus unit cost data for allocation of instructional funds. Responses to the open-ended question were consistent with the results noted above. The replies could be classified as 54 per cent favoring process data; 18 per cent favoring unit cost data and 28 per cent indifferent or neutral. Somewhat surprisingly the larger institutions and more complex institutions were more in favor of the process data than the smaller and simpler institutions. This negates a possible hypothesis that institutions might favor process data because it is easier to generate than the cost data. The categories of institutions most in favor of process data also have the greatest availability of unit cost data. One possible explanation for favoring process data over unit cost is that process data represents variables that can be directly controlled, whereas cost data is only a flag that indicates potential problems.

This striking preference for process data to support allocation decisions should encourage us to focus more research attention toward developing an understanding of the role of various types of information in the different decision processes. The study's first monograph notes the sparsity of literature that addresses the role of what we have termed cost related data.

A final question related to allocation overlaps with a subject to be discussed in a separate section below, namely exchange of cost data. Table 28 shows the response of institutions in our sample to the question of whether instructional cost comparisons among institutions are useful for allocation decisions. For all types of institutions, 62 per cent agreed or strongly agreed while only 18 per cent disagreed or strongly disagreed. However, there was substantial variation in the response by type of institution. Major research institutions agreed or strongly agreed in 51 per cent of the responses and disagreed or strongly disagreed in 20 per cent while the baccalaureate institutions agreed or strongly agreed in 71 per cent of the responses and disagreed or strongly disagreed in only 8 per cent of the responses. Perhaps the baccalaureate institutions feel that their programs are more comparable than the major research institutions do.

5.4 Management and Control

In the on-site visits we observed that the only type of control that existed at institutions was the normal periodic comparison of budgets to actual expenditures. Moreover, nearly all institutions had some form of budgetary control that monitored expenditures. While a variety of analytical approaches were used to generate reasonable expenditure rates no institution used either variable budgeting or standard costing. One institution (University of Wisconsin-La Crosse) did have a system designed to increase the frequency and detail of comparisons between the budget and actual expenditures as the end of the fiscal year approached. This seemed to be particularly effective in avoiding unauthorized expenditures.

The most important impression obtained however was the lack of interest in managerial accounting techniques. Developing a system for generating institutional institutional expenditure and are being able to explain variances between actual and planned expenditures simply did not seem to interest academic administrators. In part, the problem is that any notion of standards is difficult to promote in an academic setting. Also, the appropriate variation of costs with changes in the level of activities is not well understood.

Since there were no obvious issues to address that could be handled with a limited number of questions, no data on managerial control was collected as part of the mail survey.

5.5 Accountability

As with managerial control, the academic institutions view of accountability is somewhat limited. One important aspect of accountability is the whole area of exchange of institutional data. Information exchange is clearly associated with accountability in the minds of many administrators but the importance of the topic of information exchange has caused us to address it as a separate section below.

Based on the observations gathered during our on-site visits the primary view of accountability held by most administrators is that of fiduciary responsibility. There is little use of cost information except in gross figures such as balance sheet and operating statement data. Several of the institutions viewed the need for accountability as ad hoc and not the subject of a regular process and concern. Also, several institutions stressed a fear of the misuse of any cost data presented for accountability purposes and cited some historical examples of such misuse. This is a particularly significant problem for publicly controlled institutions.

One of the institutions visited (American University) seemed to equate accountability with openness. A serious attempt was made to have budget and cost data accessible to students, faculty, staff and the general public at American. Several of the institutions expressed interest in obtaining cost comparisons but had reservations about their validity. Many of the public institutions expected that participation in an IEP type of costing effort would be mandated in their state.

5.6 State/Federal Mandated Information

For publicly controlled institutions in particular, a major demand for cost information is the demand imposed by state and federal agencies. There are many different issues related to these external information requests. Some of the issues such as directing internal allocations and increased control of the institutions were noted above in the discussion of formulas. This section describes some of the attitudes of institutional administrators toward general issues such as overall level of load and ways to reduce it, type of unit cost data appropriate for state use, and problems related to state and federal requests for cost information.

Since the question of mandated submission of instructional unit costs has been an issue in the last several years, the mail survey contained a question that stated that the state should require submission of instructional unit costs. Table 26 shows that overall, 46 per cent of the public institutions in our sample agreed or strongly agreed with this statement while 40 per cent disagreed or strongly disagreed. This is a higher level of agreement than would generally be expected. However, the variation in response by type of institution is significant. Only 25 per cent of the public major research universities agreed or strongly agreed that the state should require submission of instructional unit costs while 59 per cent disagreed or strongly disagreed. On the other hand, 53 per cent of the public other doctoral and

TABLE 26

APPROPRIATENESS OF STATE AND FEDERAL REQUESTS FOR COST INFORMATION

	Per Cent (Public Institutions) Agree/ Strongly Agree	Per Cent (Public Institutions) Disagree/ Strongly Disagree
Your State Should Require Submission of Instructional Unit Cost Data		
All Types of Institutions	46	40
Large Institutions	39	44
Medium Size Institutions	67	28
Small Institutions	44	44
Major Research Institutions	25	59
Other Doctoral and Comprehensive Institutions	53	37
Two-year Colleges	49	34
State and Federal Agency Requests for Cost Information Are Within Reason		
All Types of Institutions	45	39
Major Research Institutions	61	33
Other Doctoral and Comprehensive Institutions	50	38
Baccalaureate Institutions	31	41
Two-year Colleges	45	43
Cost Information Required by State and Federal Agencies Is Useful for Internal Analysis		
All Types of Institutions	50	24

- -

Types of Instructional Unit Cost Data Appropriate and
Useful for State in Relation to Appropriations

Type of Data	Per Cent Identifying As Appropriate
None	15
By Level	6
By Discipline	8
By Level and Discipline	26
By Program	6
Various Other Responses	41

SOURCE: Mail Survey, Questionnaire II, Parts B and C, Questions 8, 12, 13, and 14.

comprehensive institutions agreed or strongly agreed while 37 per cent disagreed or strongly disagreed. One point to remember is that about 50 per
cent of the states use formulas to determine funding levels for the public
other doctoral and comprehensive schools. Since submission of instructional
cost data is required to establish the formulas, in these cases respondents
would simply be agreeing with what is already occurring.

In response to an open-ended question about the types of instructional
unit costs appropriate and useful for state agencies in relation to appropriations, Table 26 shows that 15 per cent of the respondents took the unusual
step of responding none. Consistent with discussions of internal availability
and usefulness in Chapter 3 above, far and away the most identified type of
instructional unit cost data is by level and discipline. Of particular
interest also is the fact that only 6 per cent of the respondents identify
program costs as appropriate for state submission. This is another indication that at this point in time, institutions simply do not show any significant support for programmatic data.

Another question in the mail survey asked whether the overall level of
requests for cost information by state and federal agencies is within reason.
Surprisingly 45 per cent of the institutions in the sample agreed or strongly
agreed while 39 per cent disagreed or strongly disagreed. Major research institutions were well above the overall average in agreeing that requests were
within reason while baccalaureate institutions were significantly below the
average level of agreement. This response that external requests are within
reason may be affected by institutions perceptions about the internal usefulness of data required by state and federal agencies. In responding to this

issue, 50 per cent of the institutions in the sample indicated agreement that
the data is useful for internal analyses while only 24 per cent expressed
disagreement. One of the institutions that we visited had made an extensive
effort to utilize the state agency database for internal analyses. This
effort failed because the state data simply did not reflect the unique categories and definitions necessary for institutional use. A related question in
the questionnaire asked if the level of external demands made it difficult to
meet internal information needs. Only 34 per cent of the responding institutions indicated that the external demand created a problem in meeting
internal information needs while 44 per cent indicated that there was no
problem. As something of a counter to this mail survey data, we should note
that several of the institutions actually visited, expressed a fear about the
future load that might be placed on them by external agencies. Also, several
of these institutions expressed a fear of the dangers of misuse of the institutional data. In particular they are leary about output measures.

Questionnaire II also included an open-ended question that asked for an
identification of ways to reduce the amount of information demanded by federal
and state agencies. Most of the respondents (47 per cent) suggested some
form of standardization and centralization of the requests. Some (7 per cent)
recommended a single line of request such as through a single state office that
all requests to institutions would have to use. Another group (16 per cent)
suggested that each request for information be accompanied by a justification
of the need for and potential use of the information.

In thinking about problems with state and federal demands we included a
question asking whether the institutions believed that technical problems

like economies of scale, stage of institutional development, program mix,
and separating research from instructional expenditures can be handled adequately in using instructional unit costs. As Table 27 indicates, only 32
per cent of the responding public institutions indicated that the technical
issues can be adequately handled while 49 per cent indicated that they cannot
be adequately handled. The medium size institutions indicate a more optimistic
response (44 per cent positive/28 per cent negative) than the average.

Another factor affecting institutional attitudes toward state and federal
demands is the extent to which the requests are viewed as being well thought
out. Table 27 shows that only 13 per cent of the responding public institutions indicate that they believe that the external agencies have a good
idea of how to use the institutional cost data that they request; 63 per cent
indicate that they do not believe that the external agencies know how to use
the data they request. In general the institutions don't believe that state
and federal agency staff members understand the nitty-gritty of institutional
management. Most of this lack of understanding is attributed to lack of
experience. There is also a belief that the level of understanding of legis-
lators and legislative analysts does not warrant extensive analysis and data
submissions. Legislative analysts say that to a large extent the requests
are a defense mechanism used by the legislature in the face of less than
candid and unclear presentations by the institutions. Institutions are
generally persuaded that the funds allocated for higher education are more
a function of state revenue levels and the general priority of higher education than a result of any cost analysis.

TABLE 27

ATTITUDES TOWARDS PROBLEMS RELATED TO STATE AND FEDERAL REQUESTS FOR COST INFORMATION

	Per Cent (Public Institutions) Agree/ Strongly Agree	Per Cent (Public Institutions) Disagree/ Strongly Disagree
The Technical Issues Involved in Using Instructional Unit Costs Can be Adequately Handled		
All Types of Institutions	32	49
Large Institutions	30	53
Medium Size Institutions	44	28
Small Institutions	28	44
Major Research Institutions	28	56
Other Doctoral and Comprehensive Institutions	35	55
Two-year Colleges	30	38

	Per Cent Agree/ Strongly Agree	Per Cent Disagree/ Strongly Disagree
The Level of External Demands Makes It Difficult to Meet Internal Information Needs		
All Types of Institutions	34	44
State and Federal Agencies Have A Good Idea of How to Use Institutional Cost Data		
All Types of Institutions	13	63
Major Research Institutions	8	77
Other Doctoral and Comprehensive Institutions	14	66
Baccalaureate Institutions	15	51
Two-year Colleges	17	55

SOURCE: Mail Survey, Questionnaire II, Parts B and C, Questions 9, 14, and 15.

The overall picture presented by the institutions is less critical than we expected regarding the overall load but somewhat more critical in terms of overcoming technical difficulties and in their assessment of the external agency staff's proper use of mandated data.

5.7 Exchange of Data

Since the advent of cost analysis in academic institutions at the beginning of this century, exchange and comparison of unit costs have been advocated as a means of providing a performance measure in academic decision making. Since academic institutions cannot use profit as a performance measure as is done in business organizations, direct comparisons are proposed. Two areas of data exchange that were of interest in almost all of the schools visited are tuition and faculty salaries. In both areas comparisons play a principal role in the decisions regarding increases. The general desire to compare cost information is reflected in responses to an open-ended question in the mail survey that indicated considerable positive sentiment regarding the usefulness of data exchange. While 37 per cent of the responses support exchange, 20 per cent were negative toward it and 30 per cent of the responses tended to be supportive but expressed reservations about obtaining truly comparable data. Of the institutions visited some questioned the value of exchanging cost data, some were enthusiastic about exchange, one had trouble in attempting to implement an exchange program, and the majority were generally interested but cautious.

Problems of comparability can come from inadequacy of the technique as well as from the selection of comparable institutions or programs. One question we asked directly was an assessment of the adequacy of the NCHEMS Information

Exchange Procedures (IEP). Table 28 shows that 21 per cent of all the

responses agreed or strongly agreed that the IEP were adequate for meaningful

exchange while 34 per cent of the respondents disagreed or strongly disagreed.

Major research universities were the type of institution most critical of IEP

(13 per cent agreed that IEP was adequate and 56 per cent disagreed). While

the IEP technique did not receive much support, the usefulness of cost compari-

sons in allocation decisions did. For all types of institutions, Table 28

shows that 62 per cent of the institutions in the mail survey agreed or strongly

agreed that cost comparisons among institutions are useful for allocation

decisions. Only 18 per cent disagreed or strongly disagreed. Table 28 also

shows some variation in the responses by type of institution with major re-

search universities showing the least support and baccalaureate institutions

showing the most. Again, the perceived homogeneity of the baccalaureate

group may be the primary factor in their more positive response.

Two other questions were included in the mail survey to get at the prob-

lems of technique inadequacies and selection of comparable schools. Both

questions stress selection of schools for comparison and use of cost related

factors for comparison rather than unit costs. Our presumption was that cost re-

lated factors such as class size and student/faculty ratios can be generated with

less problems of definition and allocation or cost assignment. In response to

a question/statement that voluntary exchange of cost related information among

selected institutions would be useful, 84 per cent of the institutions in the

sample responded favorably and only 5 per cent unfavorably. Another question/

statement addressed the relative value of comparison among selected schools

TABLE 28

USEFULNESS OF DATA EXCHANGE

	Per Cent Agree/ Strongly Agree	Per Cent Disagree/ Strongly Disagree
Voluntary Exchange of Cost Related Information Among Selected Schools Would Be Useful		
All Types of Institutions	84	5
Instructional Cost Comparisons Among Institutions Are Useful For Allocation Decisions		
All Types of Institutions	62	18
Major Research Institutions	51	20
Other Doctoral and Comprehensive Institutions	67	21
Baccalaureate Institutions	71	8
Two-year Colleges	57	15
NCHEMS IEP Procedures Are Adequate For Meaningful Exchange		
All Types of Institutions	21	34
Major Research Institutions	13	56
Other Doctoral and Comprehensive Institutions	28	35
Baccalaureate Institutions	24	18
Two-year Colleges	15	27
Comparisons of Cost and Cost Related Information Among Selected Schools Would Be More Valuable Than Comparison With National Averages	94	1

SOURCE: Mail Survey, Questionnaire II, Part D, Questions 18, 19, 20, and 21.

as opposed to the generation of national averages. Responses overwhelmingly favored comparisons with selected schools (94 per cent) as opposed to the national averages (1 per cent).

It seems that overall the support for exchange of comparative data is certainly strong. Equally clear is the institutional assessment that the techniques for comparing costs are suspect and that exchange of cost related data is more desirable. Also, the selections of the peer group against which an institution is compared is a key to its acceptability.

5.8 Observations, Conclusions, and Implications

In the sections above we have presented the data gathered through site visits to twenty-one institutions and a mail survey sent to 481 institutions as it related to the use and usefulness of cost information and cost analysis. Our review and discussion of this data highlighted a number of observations. These observations are listed here in summary form for the convenience of the reader.

- The major uses of instructional unit cost data are indirect with respect to the decision process. Primary uses are to spot problems and to increase confidence in decision making.

- Uses of unit cost data are more common in the areas of allocation and control than in the areas of acquisition and accountability.

- There is very little use of cost analysis in the area of cost recovery rate setting and tuition setting. Cost recovery is viewed as an accounting problem and tuition is a residual factor used to balance the revenues and expenses subject to competitive tuition levels.

- Enrollment or some measure of institutional load is more important than cost information in estimating and justifying funding requirements.

- States with a strong executive branch seem to prefer formula subsidy determination while strong legislative states prefer a line item and specific institution approach.

- Public institutions do not necessarily agree that support formulas should be based on cost analysis. Factors not currently handled in cost analyses may be important.

- Most public institutions feel that formula support increases state control of the institution and tends to direct internal allocations.

- Possible advantages of formula support (reduced request effort, more time for internal management, and more certain planning) were not responded to favorably by public institutions.

- Cost is not a dominant consideration in most allocation decisions. Program completeness, program quality, institutional priorities, and interpersonal relations frequently are more important than cost.

- Load is a major consideration in many allocation decisions.

- Managerial style is an important determinant of the role of cost analysis in allocation decisions.

- Cost related data (class size, faculty workload, student/ faculty ratios, and faculty salary rate) are preferred to unit cost data in supporting allocation decisions.

- Public institutions favor SCH as a measure of activity to a much greater extent than private institutions.

- Institutions are somewhat ambivalent about the usefulness of ICLM data in supporting allocation decision making.

- Institutions show a very clear preference for cost data related to level and discipline as opposed to cost data related to programs or degrees.

- There is a general lack of interest among institutions in managerial cost accounting. There is currently a serious lack of understanding in relating appropriate cost changes to changes in the level of activities.

- Most institutions do not think of accountability in terms of a regular process. Cost analysis plays almost no role in the current efforts of institutions to demonstrate their accountability.

- Institutions are not generally complaining about an overload of state and federal requests for cost information although there is some fear about future request levels.

- The major concern of institutions regarding mandated cost submissions is the inexperience of the state and federal staff personnel, a lack of understanding of the use of requested data, and possible misuse of the data.

- Institutions do not think that programmatic data should be used by state agencies in considering funding levels.

- Most institutions do not believe that the technical problems (economies of scale, stage of institutional development, program mix, and separation of research and instruction) can be adequately handled in using instructional unit cost data for appropriation decisions.

- Institutions do not believe that cost analyses are a significant factor in determining the levels of public support that they receive.

- Comparative data is a major factor affecting decision processes in the area of faculty salaries and tuition.

- Institutions generally support the concept of exchanging cost data. They seem to prefer the exchange of cost related data to exchanging unit costs and they clearly favor selection of the peer institutions for comparison.

- The institutions assessed NCHEMS IEP as inadequate for meaningful exchange. Major research universities were particularly critical in their evaluation.

In summary the above analysis and review seems to substantiate the following points:

1. Cost data and analysis is important in institutional decision making but it is not a dominant consideration. Its importance to the institution may depend on the managerial style of the institution and the relative role of the state executive and legislative branches.

2. Knowledge of cost related data or data regarding the factors
    affecting the cost of the instructional process is preferred
    to unit cost data both in internal decision processes such
    as allocation and for exchange of data with other institutions.

3. Institutions show considerable interest and support for the
    exchange of cost and cost related information. However there
    are major concerns over the techniques used and the selection
    of institutions for comparison.

4. While state agencies may want programmatic data, institutions
    are clearly most interested in generating and submitting data
    categorized by level and discipline.

Based on our review of the data we have collected, the following impli-

cations and recommendations are offered for institutions.

1. Before generating cost data, it is important to understand
    the current and expected role of cost information in specific
    decision processes. An understanding of the relative role
    of cost data in the decision making process may influence
    the analysis.

2. Careful consideration of cost related information is important.
    It has the advantage of indicating problems and identifying
    the status of important decision variables at the same time.

3. More consideration needs to be given to the area of managerial
    control.

4. It is important to recognize and address the state's frequent
    preference for programmatic data and the institution's frequent
    preference for data categorized by discipline and student level.

5. Consideration needs to be given to the possible lack of experience
    and training of state agency and legislative staff personnel as
    well as institutional staff.

6. NCHEMS IEP procedure has not been found acceptable by many
    institutions particularly the major research institutions.
    Evaluation of its potential use should be done carefully and
    thoroughly.

CHAPTER 6.0

SUMMARY, OVERALL OBSERVATIONS
AND CONCLUSIONS

In the preceding chapters we have reviewed and analyzed the institutional availability of various types of cost data and cost analysis information (Chapter 3), institutional experience with and administrators attitudes toward the production of cost information (Chapter 4), and the perceptions of institutional administrators regarding the use and usefulness of various types of cost information and analysis. This chapter contains a summary of the observations, conclusions, and implications made in Chapters 3, 4, and 5. In addition, we have developed a number of overall conclusions and implications based on the combined consideration of the observations in the three separate areas (availability, production, and use). For convenience the summaries of the observations, conclusions and implications of the separate areas are identified separately.

6.1 Institutional Availability of Data

6.1.1 Observations

- In terms of availability there is a clear ranking of types of data with student data first, faculty data second and cost data last or least available.

- Two-year colleges have a relatively low availability of student data by course level.

121

- A relatively large proportion of liberal arts institutions and two-year colleges have data files that are not even partially in machine readable form.

- All types of institutions have a relatively low availability of student data by major or degree.

- Other doctoral and comprehensive institutions and two-year colleges have a low availability of faculty data identified by rank.

- Faculty activity data is relatively unavailable in liberal arts and two-year institutions.

- Machine readability of faculty data files is relatively uncommon particularly in liberal arts and two-year institutions.

- The availability of faculty data by contact hour is relatively high particularly in two-year institutions.

- Integration of data files is a significant problem for all institutions but the level of integration is twice as high in the major research and other doctoral and comprehensive institutions as it is in the liberal arts and two-year institutions.

- Availability of ICLM data is relatively low in the liberal arts and two-year institutions.

- Marginal cost data is almost non-existent in all types of institutions. However, it appears to have a high priority for future development.

- The allocation of indirect costs to programs of instruction is available in relatively few institutions. However, it appears to have a high priority for future development.

6.1.2 Implications

1. Institutions (with the exception of the liberal arts group) like to measure their instructional activity in SCH or student contact hours by discipline. Output related measures of activity such as by major or by degree are not popular and will have to be "sold" to institutions if they are to be used.

2. Computer systems use will be impeded in many institutions because of the lack of machine readable data
   and the lack of file integration.

3. Development work on marginal cost techniques will be
   valued highly in the near future.

4. The unavailability of faculty activity data in the
   liberal arts and two-year institutions will make it
   difficult for them to develop mechanisms for allocating costs to programs.

6.2 The Production of Cost Information

6.2.1 Observations

* Systems were selected for many different reasons. In
  many cases the system development was viewed as an
  experiment supported by outside resources. All types
  of persons influenced the selection.

* Less aggregated systems (CAMPUS and RRPM) took longer
  to install and encountered more difficulties than
  highly aggregated systems.

* Homemade systems encountered less difficulty in development and provided greater perceived benefits for internal
  decisions than vendor supplied systems.

* Major development problems in the order of their frequency
  of occurrence include: input data, computer programming
  and lack of technical expertise, and poor administrative
  support and user resistance.

* Staff personnel generally handled system development and
  installation. Academic officers in particular had little
  involvement in systems development.

* Reports of financial projection models were usually
  limited to internal distribution whereas reports of
  historical cost systems were distributed both internally
  and externally. This reflects the institution's interest
  in future financial condition and the state's interest in
  accountability.

- There was wide variation in the perceived benefits from systems that produce cost information. While some institutions perceived great benefit other institutions perceived no tangible good from their use. In particular, CAMPUS systems studied seemed to have no impact on institutional decision making. About half of the users of IEP and/or RRPM indicate that the benefits have outweighed the costs.

- For financial projections, highly aggregated systems such as PLANTRAN and SEARCH tended to be much more useful than the more disaggregate RRPM and CAMPUS systems.

6.2.2 Implications

1. Institutions should identify in advance of systems development the specific needs and uses for systems in addition to general needs.

2. Users, in particular academic officers, should become more involved in system design.

3. Institutions should consider highly aggregated cost projection systems. Cost projection models should be built from the top down and expanded in an evolutionary fashion as needed.

4. Alternative systems should be identified and carefully considered.

5. For historical costing or large financial projection systems, an institution should expect to devote considerable effort in improving input data and in installing the system on the computer.

6. Administrators should recognize that it is very difficult (and perhaps impossible) in most cases to meet external needs and internal needs for data from the same system.

7. Homemade systems should be considered for internal decision making, particularly if information needs have not been carefully identified.

8. Vendors and institutional staffs should be encouraged to provide modeling services, such as, identifying information needs, user education, and analysis of model outputs as well as supplying models.

9.   Systems development efforts should concentrate on changing decision processes and decision making styles as well as on model installation.

10.   Institutions should consider a staged plan to improve the use of cost information.

6.3   Institutional Use of Cost Information

6.3.1   Observations

- The major uses of instructional unit cost data (spot problems, increase confidence in decision making) are indirect with respect to the decision making process.

- Uses of unit cost data are more common in the areas of allocation and control than in the areas of acquisition and accountability.

- There is very little use of cost analysis in the areas of cost recovery rate setting and tuition setting.

- Enrollment or some measure of institutional load is more important than cost information in estimating and justifying funding requirements.

- States with a strong executive branch seem to prefer formula subsidy determination while strong legislative states prefer a line item by institution approach.

- Public institutions do not necessarily agree that support formulas should be based on cost analysis. Other factors such as equity, available state resources and priorities are important.

- Most public institutions feel that formula support increases state control of the institution and tends to direct internal allocations.

- Public institutions did not respond favorably to possible advantages of formula support (reduced request effort, more time for internal management, and more certain planning).

- Cost is not a dominant consideration in most allocation decisions. Program completeness, program quality, institutional priorities, and interpersonal relations frequently are more important than cost.

- Load is a major consideration in many allocation decisions.

- Managerial style is an important determinant of the role of cost analysis in allocation decisions.

- Cost related data (class size, faculty workload, student/faculty ratios, and faculty salary rate) are preferred to unit cost data in supporting allocation decisions.

- Public institutions favor SCH as a measure of activity to a much greater extent than private institutions.

- Institutions are somewhat ambivalent about the usefulness of ICLM data in supporting allocation decision making.

- Institutions clearly prefer cost data related to level and discipline as opposed to cost data related to programs or degrees.

- There is a general lack of interest among institutions in managerial cost accounting.

- Cost analysis plays almost no role in the current efforts of institutions to demonstrate their accountability; accountability is not viewed as a regular process at most institutions.

- While there is some fear regarding future requirements, institutions are generally not complaining about an overload of state and federal requests for cost information.

- Institutions are concerned about the lack of experience of the state and federal staff personnel, their lack of understanding regarding the use of requested data, and possible misuse of the data.

- Institutions do not think that programmatic data should be used by state agencies in considering funding levels.

- Most institutions do not believe that technical problems can be adequately handled in using in- structional unit cost data for appropriation decisions.

- Institutions do not believe that cost analyses are a signficant factor in determining the levels of public support that they receive.

- Comparative data is a major factor affecting decisions regarding faculty salaries and tuitions.

- Institutions support the concept of data exchange. They prefer the exchange of cost related data to exchanging unit costs and they favor selection of peer institutions for comparison rather than the use of broad categories.

- Most institutions assessed NCHEMS IEP as inadequate for meaningful exchange. Major research universities were particularly critical in their evaluation.

6.3.2 Implications

1. Before generating cost data, it is important to under- stand the current and expected role of cost infor- mation in specific decision processes. An understanding of the relative role of cost data in the decision making process may influence the analysis.

2. Careful consideration of cost related data is important. It has the advantage of indicating problems and identi- fying the status of important decision variables at the same time.

3. More consideration needs to be given to the area of mana- gerial control.

4. It is important to recognize and address the state's prefer- ence for programmatic data and the institution's frequent preference for data categorized by discipline and student level.

5. Consideration needs to be given to the possible lack of experience and training of state agency and legislative staff personnel.

6. Evaluation of the use of NCHEMS IEP procedure should
   be done carefully and thoroughly. Most institutions,
   particularly the major research ones, have not found
   it acceptable.

In reviewing the observations and implications from the three areas,
i.e., availability, production, and use, we see some reinforcing and comple-
mentary patterns that suggest some overall or integrative observations, conclusions, and recommendations. Some of these overall impressions are noted
below.

6.4 Overall (Integrative) Observations

- The heterogeneous nature of higher education is evident. Differences in the extent of machine readability
  and integration of data files and the appropriateness
  of using SCH as a measure of institutional activity
  are important in the handling of each type of institution. The relative success of homemade systems can
  be attributed to their ability to overcome the
  problems of heterogeneity.

- State and federal needs for cost information are somewhat counter, at least in terms of priorities, with
  the needs of the institution. State interests in historical cost analyses and in programmatic categories
  are different from institutional interest in projection of aggregate totals and in data categorized
  by level and discipline.

- Available information, current systems and the current
  level of administrative expertise all suggest that the
  processes of internal management are not being given
  significant emphasis.

- The current institutional view of accountability is
  limited. Appropriate information elements need to be
  defined and systems developed that address this
  potential need.

6.5 Recommendations

1. A major research effort should be undertaken to better define the decision making environment in higher education. We must know a great deal more about what decisions are being made, who is making decisions, how are decisions being made and what information is supporting the decision making processes. Further it would be helpful to have a realistically based concept of how the decision processes should operate. Wyatt and Zeckhauser [1975] give an example of the needed type of research.

2. Managerially oriented tools need to be developed. NACUBO's work with fixed and variable costing is a strong step in the right direction. A clear treatment of marginal cost with some discussion of methodology is needed.

3. Educational opportunities for the staff personnel of state and federal agencies as well as at institutions need to be developed. The first monograph raised the issue of educational programs on the basis of literature needs. Data and analysis in this monograph suggest the same needs on the basis of current conditions.

4. External and internal information needs must be placed in juxtaposition and compared. There is an impression that suggests that in large part, both external and internal decision makers need the same data. Our study and analysis suggest that this impression is false. Careful analysis is needed.

5. More work should be done on categorizing institutions for different purposes. Policy issues affect different segments of higher education differently. Current categorization schemes do not adequately reflect different aspects of the institutions.

REFERENCES

Adams, Carl R., R. L. Hankins and Roger G. Schroeder, The Literature of Cost Analysis in Higher Education, Monograph 1 of Study of Cost Analysis in Higher Education Project, University of Minnesota, Minneapolis, MN, March 1977.

Benacerraf, Paul, W. G. Bowen, T. A. Davis, W. W. Lewis, L. K. Morse and C. W. Schafer, "Budgeting and Resource Allocation at Princeton University," Report to Ford Foundation, Princeton, New Jersey, June 1972.

Clark, David G., et al., "Introduction to RRPM 1.6," NCHEMS, Boulder, Colorado, Technical Report 34A, 1973.

Johnson, Richard and Robert Huff, "Information Exchange Procedures," NCHEMS, Boulder, Colorado, Technical Report 65, January 1975.

Judy, Richard W., "Systems Analysis for Efficient Resource Allocation in Higher Education, Minter and Lawrence (eds.), Management Information Systems: Their Development and Use in Higher Education, WICHE, Boulder, Colorado, October 1969.

Keane, G. F. and J. N. Daniel, "Systems for Exploring Alternative Resource Commitments in Higher Education, (SEARCH)," Peat, Marwick and Mitchell, 1970.

Midwest Research Institute, "An Introduction to PLANTRAN II," Kansas City, Missouri (n.d.).

Midwest Research Institute, "PLANTRAN II: Computer Assisted Institutional Research and Planning," Kansas City, Missouri, 1972.

Romney, Leonard, "Information Exchange Procedures, Overviews and General Approach," NCHEMS, Boulder, Colorado, Technical Report 28, September 1972.

Schroeder, Roger G. (ed.), Site Visit Descriptions of Costing Systems and Their Use in Higher Education, Monograph 3 of Study of Cost Analysis in Higher Education Project, University of Minnesota, Minneapolis, MN, March 1977.

Systems Research Group, "CAMPUS VIII Planning Model," Toronto, Canada, October 1972.

Weathersby, George, "The Development and Applications of a University Cost Simulation Model," Graduate School of Business Administration and Office of Analytic Studies, University of California, Berkeley, June 15, 1967.

Wyatt, Joe B. and Sally Zeckhauser, "University Executives and Management Information: A Tenuous Relationship," Educational Record 56 (1975): 175-89.

APPENDIX 1

CONDENSED USER INTERVIEW GUIDE

Section I.   Background Material

    Summary: This section contains the background material such as
the information forwarded from the campus liaison as
well as any relevant correspondence between the interviewer and the various interviewees. In addition,
included is an interviewer outline.

Section II.   User Provides a Detailed Description of Cost Information and
Analysis Used in Decision Process.

    Summary: Each part of this section will trace the cost information
and cost analysis used in a specific decision process.
It will include an evaluation of the data and techniques
employed in the process, as well as the changes anticipated or desired.

In addition, it will also include the background of the
users being interviewed.

Part I.   Acquisition of Funds

    1.   Appropriation Income Justification (Public)
    2.   Estimation of Aggregate Operating Budget (Private)
    3.   Tuition Setting
    4.   Cost Recovery Rate Determination
    5.   Gift and/or Endowment Income Projection
    6.   Other

Part II.   Allocation of Available Resources

    1.   Allocation to Major Budget Categories (e.g., NACUBO
         Listings) at Aggregate Institutional Level
    2.   Allocation to Existing Academic Units
    3.   Adding or Dropping New Academic Units or Programs
    4.   Determine Overall Faculty Salary Levels
    5.   Other

Part III.   Management Control of Operating Budget

Part IV.   Accountability

    1.   Internal Cost Control
    2.   External Cost Control

Background of Institution

    Identification

Name   _____

Address   _____

Affiliation (control   _____

Enrollment   _____

Student Body
  (men, women, coed)   _____

Institutional Documents   √ if we have

Organizational Chart   ____

Catalogue   ____

Constitution, Bylaws and Regulations   ____

Faculty and Staff Manuals   ____

Chart of Accounts   ____

President's Reports - Annual
  Statistical Summary   ____

Budgeting Calendar   ____

Budgets Formats and Budget Instruction   ____

Special Studies Inculding Cost Analysis   ____

Planning Documents   ____

<u>Background of Individual</u> (for each user interviewed)

Job Title_____ Name_____

As you know, administrators have widely varied backgrounds with respect to education and experience. We would like to get a clear picture of your background with respect to the following areas.

Degrees	Major	Location	Year
_____	_____	_____	_____
_____	_____	_____	_____
_____	_____	_____	_____
_____	_____	_____	_____

Would you please indicate the experience you have had in the following areas.

<u>Type of Contact</u>

Subject	Courses	Short Courses	Extensive Reading	Job Experience
Institutional Research				
Accounting				
Management or Administration				
Operations Research or Management Science				
Economics				
Industrial Engineering				

In each box checked above, please make a numerical correspondence with the detailed description given below.

Please go back and explain the topics covered and the sources of the courses, readings, and job experience (type and how long).

| | Type of Contact | | |
Specific Material	Short Courses	Extensive Reading	Job Experience
Resource Requirements Prediction Model (RRPM)			
Comprehensive Analytical Methods for Planning in University Systems (CAMPUS)			
System for Evaluating Alternative Commitments in Higher Education (SEARCH)			
Higher Education Long Range Planning/Planning Translation (HELP/PLANTRAN)			
National Center for Higher Education Management Information Systems' - Information Exchange Procedure (NCHEMS-IEP)			
Program Classification Structure (PCS)			
Planning Programming Budgeting Systems (PPBS)			
Standard Costing			
Marginal Costing			
Cost Simulation Models			
Cost Accounting Models			

As you did before, please number the boxes to correspond with their description below.

Please go back and explain the topics covered and the sources of the courses, readings, and job experience (type and how long).

Introduction

The purpose of this project is to develop a profile of the impact of cost information and cost analysis on institutional decision making. To do this, the Study of Cost Analysis in Higher Education group is conducting in-depth interviews with 21 colleges of various sizes and classifications who are "experienced" in the production and use of cost information and cost analysis.

To get a clear picture of the interrelationship between information and analysis in decision making, we have chosen a decision-use-framework for collecting and analyzing information about costing as it is used by decision makers in specific decision situations. We hope that this approach will allow us to compare the value of cost information and cost analysis per se with the importance of non-cost information and analysis in each of the decision processes.

We identify four major categories of institutional decision making activities: (1) acquisition of funds, (2) allocation of available resources, (3) management and control, and (4) accountability.

We would like to discuss these decision processes with you in one of two manners determined by how familiar you are with the subject matter. The first alternative is to discuss one of the four major categories on an aggregate level, not focusing on any specific decision. This approach might best be taken if there are no independent decisions to be made in the process. It might then be described as a succession of events. We would want you to outline the major sources of data and information accessed and the issues to be resolved within the process. For example, within the process of management and control, if there is no set of subprocesses which you can identify as being separate and distinct from one another and which together make up the major decision making area, we would try to approach the subject on an aggregate level.

The alternative, is to briefly outline an overview of the area of decision making, noting the set of decisions which make up that area and then to focus on detail about each of the subprocesses on an individual basis. For example, if the area of decision making is acquisition of funds and you see it as being broken into the processes of tuition setting, appropriation income justification, and gift and endowment estimation, we would like you to outline each of these processes separately.

The main interest in pursuing these approaches is to get a clear picture of the use of cost information, and cost analysis in the decision process. It is also important that we form an understanding of the value of this cost information relative to types of non-cost information in a decision process.

Do you have any questions or are you unclear on any part of our approach? If not, I would like to begin with an aggregate process which you were selected to describe.

Decision Process

I. Acquisition of Funds (in general)

Possible Subprocesses:

1. Appropriation Income Justification (Public)

2. Estimation of Aggregate Operating Budget (Private)

3. Tuition Setting

4. Cost Recovery Rate Determination

5. Gift and/or Endowment Income Projection

6. Other

II. Allocation of Available Resources (in general)

Possible Subprocesses:

1. Allocation to Major Categories (e.g., NACUBO Listings) at Aggregate Institutional Level

2. Allocation to Existing Academic Units

3. Adding or Dropping New Academic Units or Programs

4. Determine Overall Faculty Salary Levels

5. Other

III. Management Control of Operating Budget

IV. Accountability (in general)

Possible Subprocesses:

1. Internal Cost Control

2. External Cost Control

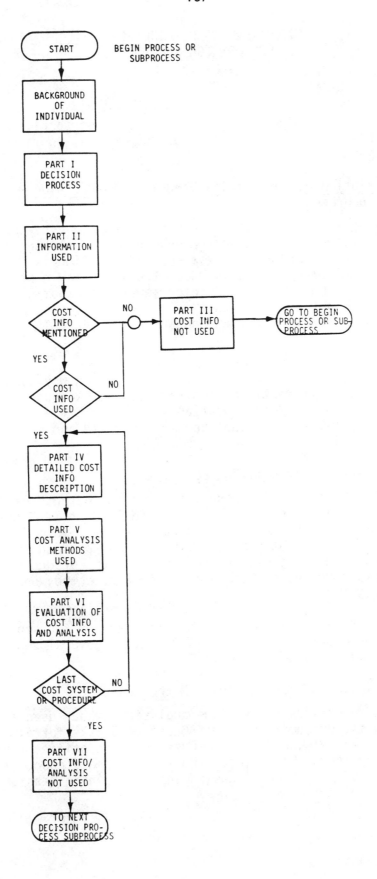

INTERVIEWER'S OUTLINE FOR EACH
PROCESS (OR SUBPROCESS)

Part I: <u>Decision Process (or Subprocess) Description</u>

In this part we would like the interviewee to give his general comments on how the process (or subprocess) operates at his institution.

Part II: <u>Description of Information Used in this Decision Process or (Subprocess)</u>

Here we are interested in both cost and non-cost types of information, preferably in some rough order of ranking if possible. If the interviewer sees that cost information is either not mentioned or not actually used, the interview continues at Part III, question #1. If the interviewer sees that cost information is mentioned and feels that it is actually used, Part III is skipped and the interview continues with Part IV.

Part III: <u>Cost Information Not Obtained or Not Used</u>

In this part, the interview focuses both on why cost information is not used currently and whether it ever was used or conceivably could be used. After question #4, the interview would go on to the next process (or subprocess). Part IV and beyond is <u>not</u> filled out.

Part IV: <u>Detailed Cost Information Description</u>

Part IV is a detailed description of the outputs used from each cost systems or procedure identified in Part II. If a description of system or procedure output has already been made, one can simply identify those outputs actually used and proceed to Part V. The notation should jibe with that used in the producer's questionnaire. If outputs have not been previously documented, one must complete Part IV.

Parts IV-VI are to be completed for each of the separate system/procedure outputs recorded in Part II. Several copies of Parts IV-VI may thus be completed.

Part V: <u>Description of Cost Analysis Method Used</u>

Part V describes the various analysis methods used and who did the analysis, producer or user. Question 5 asks for <u>all</u> analysis used regardless of who does it. Question 6 identifies that analysis done by users themselves. (Note: This is a change from the method of recording discussed in the training sessions.)

PART VI: <u>Evaluation of Cost Information/Analysis Method</u>

In this section both information and analysis are discussed together. Various evaluation questions are included. After completing Part VI, one must go back to Part IV, for each of the remaining cost procedures or systems that were originally documented in Part II. When all system/procedures have been documented by Part IV-VI, go on to Part VII.

Part VII: <u>Cost Information and Analysis Not Used</u> (Rejected or Future)

Cost Information/Analysis not used is documented here. After completing this section, go on to the next process.

Interviewee_____

Process (Subprocess)_____

QUESTIONS FOR EACH DECISION PROCESS OR SUBPROCESS

Part I.   Decision Process (or Subprocess) Description

How does this decision process (or subprocess) operate? Provide a brief description of who is involved, timing, procedures used, etc.

Part II.   Description of Information Used in this Decision Process (or Subprocess)

What types (cost and non-cost) of information are used in this decision process (or subprocess)?

a.   _____

b.   _____

c.   _____

d.   _____

e.   _____

Please roughly rank the importance of these above types of information.

[Note to Interviewer: If cost data or cost information is not mentioned then go on to Part III.]

If cost information is mentioned ascertain whether it is actually used in the decision process (or subprocess). For example, if the interviewee evidences a high degree of familiarity with the cost information this possibly indicates that the cost information is actually used. If the cost information is not used then go on to Part III. If cost information is used, then go on to Part IV.

Part III.   Cost Information Not Obtained or Not Used

1. Why do you feel that the non-cost information is important in this decision process (or subprocess) and cost information is not?

2. Was cost information for this decision process (or sub-
    process) ever obtained or used and subsequently dropped
    or rejected?   Y   N (circle one).

    If yes, what types of cost information were used or con-
    sidered for this decision process (or subprocess)?

    a. _____

    b. _____

    c. _____
    (Reference to producer system if possible.)
    If no, why were they dropped or rejected?

3. What cost information do you think you want for use in this
    decision process (or subprocess)?

    a. _____

    b. _____

    c. _____
    How would this cost information affect this decision process?

    What problem do you expect or are you having in acquiring
    this cost information?

4. In the next three to five years what changes (if any) in
    cost information relevant to this decision process (or
    subprocess) do you expect to occur? Please identify (if
    any) those which you want and those which you don't want.

    [Note to Interviewer: do not fill out subsequent ques-
    tions for this decision process (or subprocess). Go to
    the next decision process.]

Part IV. Detailed Cost Information Description

Generic cost name:_____
   (from Part II)

I. Description of Cost Information Type

If a detailed description of system or procedure outputs has
already been made, reference those output numbers that are
actually used in the decision process. Use the same output
numbers as recorded in the producer interviews. If a detailed
description has not been previously made, fill out this section
for cost information actually used.

Complete Parts IV-VI for each of the different systems or
procedures recorded in Part II. Several iterations of Parts
IV-VI may then be needed, if separate cost systems or procedures were recorded in Part II.

A. Measure of Cost   Output Measure

_____ Total*   _____ Student Credit Hour

_____ Average (per unit)   _____ Student Contact Hour

_____ Marginal/Incremental   _____ FTE Student

*no output measure required   _____ Headcount Students

                                       _____ Degree Granted

                                       _____ Other _____

                                       _____ Other _____

B. Allocation   Allocation and Basis

_____ Direct   _____

_____ Indirect (Allocated)   _____

_____ Full (Direct &   _____
          Allocated)
                                       (use the reverse side if
                                       necessary)

C. Volume Relationship (if identified)

_____ Variable

_____ Fixed

_____ Semi-variable or Mixed

D. <u>Cost Basis</u>

_____ Historical (Actual)   _____ Replacement

_____ Standard   _____ Imputed

_____ Estimated (Projected)

basis of projection: historical _____

                       other   _____

E. <u>Subject of Costing</u>

_____ Organizational Unit (e.g., department, college, etc.)

_____ Program (e.g., major, degree, research output)

_____ Program/Function (e.g., instruction, research,
         service, etc.)

_____ Activity (e.g., discipline, course, research project,
         scheduled teaching, advising)

_____ Object of Cost (e.g., faculty salaries, supplies, etc.)

Description of each entry above:
(Identify by procedure number if there is more than one
output; record a description for <u>each</u> output above.)

_____

_____

_____

_____

_____

_____

_____

F. Additional Descriptive Comments

_____

_____

_____

_____

[Note to interviewer: go on to Part V.]

Part V.   Description of Cost Analysis Method Used

5.   Which of the following methods of cost analysis are used in this process. Record all analyses used, whether provided by producers or done by users themselves. Describe the method used. Identify types of data used in the analysis.

a.   percentages or ratios of cost elements.

b.   comparisons (over time perhaps) of cost against budget or standards or between institutions.

c.   comparisons of costs between decision alternatives.

d.   cost-volume analysis.

e.   break-even analysis (cost-volume-revenue relationships).

f.   other

6.   We want to separate those methods of cost analysis which are performed by users, such as yourself, from those methods which are provided by producers in finished form.

Identify [with a * above (in question 5)] those methods of cost analysis that are performed entirely or for the most part by users, after the information is transmitted to them.

Part VI.   Evaluation of Cost Information/Analysis Method

In this part and the next part we are referring to the cost information and the cost analysis method combined. If the experience with the cost information differs from the experience with the analysis method, split your answers in each such questions.

7.   Who determined the content and form of this cost information/ analysis method? Characterize role of producer versus user.

8.   Briefly describe why this type of cost information/analysis method was selected?

9.   Characterize the role of this cost information/analysis method in the decision process (or subprocess). What is the relative importance of the cost information and analysis used and what actual and potential impact does it have on this decision process (or subprocess)? Is it necessary?

10.   What problems have been encountered in obtaining and using this cost information/analysis (e.g., lack of producer knowledge, lack of user knowledge, user resistance, time- liness, lack of funds, misuse of data)?

11. Of these problems which were the most important to overcome?

12. Have these problems been overcome? If so, how? If not, why not?

Go back to Part IV, if all cost systems or procedures originally listed in Part II have not been documented by Parts IV-VI.

Part VII. Cost Information and Analysis Not Used (Rejected or Future)

13. Was other cost information or cost analysis ever obtained or used for this decision process (or subprocess) and subsequently dropped or rejected?   Y   N (circle one)

If yes, what types of other cost information or cost analysis methods were used or considered for this decision process (or subprocess)?

a. _____

b. _____

c. _____

If no, why were they dropped or rejected?

14. Can you conceive of any other cost or cost analysis method which would actually be of use in this decision process (or subprocess)? Y   N (circle one)

If yes, what are they?

a. _____

b. _____

c. _____

If yes, how would this other cost information or analysis method affect this decision process?

If yes, what problems do you expect in acquiring this other cost information/analysis?

15. In the next three to five years what changes (if any) in cost information or analysis relevant to this decision process (or subprocess) do you expect to occur? Please identify (if any) those which you want and those which you don't want.

APPENDIX 2

CONDENSED SYSTEMS (PRODUCERS) INTERVIEW GUIDE

Part I.

The purpose of these interviews is to identify and gather information on procedures and systems which produce cost-analytic information for your institution or various constituencies. The procedures or systems will be limited to those associated with instructional, research or service costing.

For this study we have defined a procedure as: a set of instructions which specifies (1) a set of tasks to be performed by certain individuals and/or machines; (2) the sequence in which the tasks are to be performed; and (3) the data elements necessary to produce a single desired analytic output measure. We define a system as: an integrated set of procedures which produces more than one separately identifiable analytic output measure. For example, a procedure may generate the direct costs of instruction per student credit hour by discipline as its only output. A system, in contrast, may generate as one output the direct cost of instruction per student credit hour by discipline and, as a second output, the direct costs of instruction per student credit hour by level of course. Frequently there may be one or more common dimensions shared by separate analytic outputs.

Our initial task will be to identify those cost-analytic procedures and/or systems for which you and your staff are responsible. From that list we will select those about which we will wish to gather data on development and implementation. More specifically, the procedures and/or systems in which we are primarily interested are (1) output related (unit or average) instructional cost calculations, (2) projections of operating budget requirements, (3) allocations of indirect costs, (4) cost-volume revenue relationship analyses, (5) program budgeting analyses, and (6) cost analysis of research or service. We are not focusing on procedures and/or systems which generate routine accounting ledgers or budget statements, except as these may contain significant unique features which facilitate analytical efforts. We shall ask your help in identifying these.

We recognize that you may describe or refer to a procedure or system in a manner which does not fully characterize its output(s). Since our staff will categorize the information we gather according to the description of output data, we will need your help in making the cross-over from your terminology. For example, you may use a system which you call a Cost Estimation Model and which produces the following four outputs: (1) required teaching faculty by rank; (2) student credit hours by level and discipline; (3) direct costs by object of expense and discipline; and (4) annual direct costs per student credit hour by level and discipline. It will be necessary for us to categorize this system by the descriptions of these four outputs. It should be borne in mind, however, that the questions we will ask regarding development and implementation will refer to the integrated system rather than the sub-system procedures.

(Instructions for staff and campus liaison)

Based on the foregoing explanation, please list below the cost analytic procedures (systems) that are or have been in use at this institution and those under development. Include procedures that are entirely manual, partially computerized or entirely computerized.

a. _____

b. _____

c. _____

d. _____

e. _____

(use reverse of this sheet if necessary)

For each of the cost information systems or procedures you have identified we would like to have you describe in general terms the evolutionary process that brought you to your present system. For example, the current output might be the result of a single integrated development or a series of small improvements over time. There may have been more output generated at one time than you now use.

1. In general terms please describe the historical development of the present day system.

2. In general terms please describe your future plans for developing or modifying your costing systems or procedures.

Part II.   Procedure (System) Output and Operation

(To be completed for each procedure (system) selected for investigation)

A. Description of Procedure (System) Output

Institution _____

1. Name of procedure or system_____

2. Name of person to be interviewed about the procedure or system

_____

3. Production Unit _____

4. Cost data outputs of the procedure or system.

For purposes of categorization and analysis we will characterize each procedure or system according to the description of its data output (e.g., direct cost of instruction per student credit hour by major and level). If a single output procedure is being described, check (√) each distinguishing characteristic of the output. If a multiple output system is being described, enter a "1" by each distinguishing characteristic common to a single output (e.g., direct cost of instruction per student credit hour by major); enter a "2" by each distinguishing characteristic common to a second single output (e.g., direct cost of instruction per student credit hour by major and level); enter "3" by each distinguishing characteristic common to the third separate output, etc. Note that separate outputs may have common distinguishing characteristics.

A. Measure of Cost   Output Measure

___ Total*   ___ Student Credit Hour

___ Average (per unit)   ___ Student Contact Hour

___ Marginal/Incremental   ___ FTE Student (Major)

                                   ___ Headcount Students

* no output measure required   ___ Degree Granted

                                   ___ Other _____

                                   ___ Other _____

B. <u>Allocation</u>   <u>Allocation and Basis</u>

   ___ Direct   _____

   ___ Indirect (Allocated)   _____

   ___ Full (Direct & Indirect)   _____
                                             (use reverse side if necessary)

C. <u>Volume Relationship</u> (If Identified)

   ___ Variable

   ___ Fixed

   ___ Semi-Variable or Mixed

D. <u>Cost Basis</u>

   ___ Historical Actual   ___ Replacement

   ___ Standard   ___ Imputed

   ___ Estimated (Projected) - basis of projection

                                     ____ historical

                                     ____ other _____

E. <u>Subject of Costing</u>

   ___ Organizational Unit (e.g., department, college, etc.)

   ___ Program (e.g., major, degree, research output)

   ___ Program/Function (e.g., instruction, research, service, etc.)

   ___ Activity (e.g., discipline, course, research project, scheduled
            teaching, advising)

   ___ Object of Cost (e.g., faculty salaries, supplies, etc.)

Description of each entry above:
(Identify by procedure number if there is more than one output; record
a description for <u>each</u> output above)

_____

_____

_____

_____

_____

_____

_____

F. Additional Descriptive Comments

_____

_____

_____

_____

Part II. B. Description of Procedure (System) Operation

(To be read to interviewee)

In this section we would like to learn in some detail the manner in which this procedure (system) operates.

5. Characterize the input to the procedure in terms of types of data required. [registration, budget, faculty assignment or activity.]

6. Please explain the algorithmic components of the procedure. What is the basis for the conversion of inputs into outputs? E.g., average or maximum class size, type of faculty activity, student flow, etc.

7. To what degree is this procedure (system) computerized, manual or a combination of both. Please explain what function the computer plays and what is done manually.

8. How frequently is this procedure (system) run, and when is it run?

(If the procedure (system) described is manual go to question 10.)

9. Is this procedure (system) run by batch processing or on-line? If on-line, please indicate the types of terminals used and the users' reactions (positive or negative) to using those terminals. Please indicate the amount of input/output done on-line.

10. Describe the computing facility upon which this procedure (system) is run. Include the make and model number of the computer, core size, type of secondary storage that you rely on (tape, random access). Indicate if the computer is located at your school. If it is not, who provides computer services for you.

11. If this procedure (system) was obtained from a source outside your institution, indicate the approximate number of man hours that were spent revising it for your use. What kinds of changes were made? Did you expect all of these revisions to be necessary?

12. Please check the responses below which best describe the condition of the database for this procedure (system) when it was installed.

13. Describe any changes, additions, corrections that had to be made to the data to get it in the required form and format for this procedure (system). Approximately how many man-hours were spent performing this function? Was the procedure (system) changed so that it might conform to existing data? If yes, explain.

    The data were:

    a. in the appropriate machine readable form   __/ __/ __/ __/

    b. in the correct format   __/ __/ __/ __/

    c. complete in terms of numbers of records   __/ __/ __/ __/

    d. integrated to extent needed with other data   __/ __/ __/ __/

14. a. Please describe the previous experience that the staff had in developing and implementing this type of a procedure or procedures that were similar.

    b. Also to what extent did such previous experience contribute to a reduction in man hours required to develop and implement this particular procedure? None _____ Some _____ Much _____ Very Much _____

15. a. For computerized procedures describe the general competence or sophistication that the staff had in the systems design and programming area.

    b. Indicate the extent to which this general competence may have contributed to a reduction in man hours required to develop and implement this particular procedure? None _____ Some _____ Much _____ Very Much _____

Part III. Selection of the Procedure (System)

(To be read to interviewee)

In this section we would like to learn about conditions, events, and principal persons involved in the decision to select this particular procedure (system).

16. What needs, desires or pressures within your institution brought about the selection of this procedure (system)?

17. Please identify any individuals, organizations and/or conditions external to your institution which influenced this selection and indicate the role each played.

18. What specific problem(s) was the procedure (system) intended to address?

Selection of the Procedure (System) Continued

19. Was this procedure (system) intended to supplement an existing procedure (system)? to replace one? If yes, please explain.

20. What was the source of this procedure (system)? (e.g., purchased from, adapted or copied from, developed internally.)

21. When did you initiate the selection process which resulted in your institution choosing this procedure (system)?

Selection of the Procedure (System) Continued

22. Please describe the major events in this selection process.

23. Who was involved in consultation, discussion, etc. regarding the needs of your institution as they might be met through the selection of this procedure (system)?

24. a. Please describe any alternative procedures (systems) or courses of action that were considered.

    b. What drawbacks or shortcomings, if any, regarding the rejected procedures (systems) were identified during the selection process?

Selection of the Procedure (System) Continued

25. Why was this particular procedure (system) selected?

26. What drawbacks or shortcomings, if any, regarding the selected procedure (system) were identified during the selection process?

27. Who made the actual decision to select this procedure (system) and on what basis was that decision made?

Part IV.   Development and Installation of the Procedure (System)

(To be read to interviewees)

In this section we would like to learn about the conditions, events and principal persons involved in the development and installation of the procedure (system). (This includes the elapsed time from the selection of the procedure (system) until it reached operational status.)

28.   Describe the sequence of events involved in developing and installing this procedure (system). (Names of 4 or 5 major milestones.)

29.   Who was involved in the development and installation of this procedure (system)?

30.   What role did persons from outside your institution play in the development and installation of this procedure (system)?

31.   Please identify any major problems encountered in development and installation (include technical, administrative, financial, political, etc.).

(If no major problems are identified, omit question 32.)

32.   Were these problems anticipated? If not, why not?

33.   If this procedure (system) was purchased or developed externally for your institution, did the installation take place according to your expectations? If not, what went wrong?

34.   Was there any change in your institution's needs as related to this procedure (system) during the development and installation phase? If yes, what modifications in the procedure (system) resulted?

35.   Were there any changes in your institution's expectations for the procedure (system) during development and installation? If yes, what modifications resulted?

36.   How much time elapsed between the selection of the procedure (system) and the point at which it was fully operational (i.e., as in IIA)?

37.   How much time elapsed between the selection of the procedure (system) and the first output of usable data from the procedure (system)?

38.   Describe what information was available as the first usable output.

(If the procedure (system) is under development but not yet operational, omit remainder of questionnaire.)

154

Part V. <u>Operation and Evaluation of the Procedure (System)</u>

    (To be read to interviewee)

In this section we would like to learn about conditions, events and principal persons involved in the operation of the procedure (system) if it is
or has been operational.

    39. Is this procedure (system) currently operational? Has it been
         operational at some time in the past but subsequently discontinued?
         (approximate date)

(If the procedure (system) was discontinued prior to becoming operational,
go to Section VI.)

    40. In general terms, what is (was) the distribution list for the
         output of this procedure (system)?

    41. In what way, if any, are (were) you or your staff "users" of the
         output of this procedure (system)?

    42. What benefits do you identify as resulting from the use of this
         procedure (system)?

    43. In your judgment, is (was) the level of benefit adequate in
         terms of its cost? Please explain your answer.

    44. In what way, if any, do you believe that use of this procedure
         (system) has affected administrative decision-making within your
         institution?

    45. Please indicate how well use of this procedure (system) met <u>your</u>
         expectations in terms of its logic, data input requirements and
         outputs.

    46. If this procedure (system) has failed to meet <u>your</u> expectations
         in terms of logic, data input requirements and outputs, what
         reasons do you give?

    47. What is your impression of how well this procedure (system) met
         the expectations of the person or persons (other than yourself)
         who selected it in terms of its logic, data input requirements
         and outputs.

    48. If you feel this procedure (system) has failed to meet the expec-
         tations of the person or persons who selected it, do you believe
         this to be the result of a failure to understand or evaluate
         adequately the needs of the institution? the procedure (system)
         itself?

49. What, if any, major changes in this procedure (system) were made subsequent to its becoming operational? Why?

50. What, if any, major changes in processing are anticipated? Why?

51. Give your overall evaluation of this procedure (system). (Criteria for evaluation must be included.)

Part VI. Discontinued Procedures (Systems)

In this section we would like to learn what factors entered into the discontinuation of a procedure (system) which was dropped either during development and installation or after it became operational.

52. If this procedure (system) has been discontinued, at what point is its development and installation or operation was the decision made?

53. What was the basis for the decision to discontinue the procedure (system)?

54. Who were the people involved in making this decision and what were their roles?

55. What, if any, procedure (system) has your institution selected to take its place?

STAGES OF SYSTEM DEVELOPMENT AND OPERATIONS

Cost Categories	Definition (feasibility study, information needs)		Development & Installation (system design, programs, manuals, procedures)		Operations (operations + maintenance)	
I. PERSONNEL	CODE	TOTAL RESOURCES	CODE	TOTAL RESOURCES	CODE	ANNUAL RESOURCES
		DOLLARS / MAN HRS.		DOLLARS / MAN HRS.		DOLLARS / MAN HRS.
a) Producers						
• Supervisory		$		$		$
• Technical						
• Clerical						
b) Capturers of Data		DOLLARS / HRS.		DOLLARS / HRS.		DOLLARS / HRS.
• Clerical		XXXXXXXX / XXXX				
• Faculty		XXXXXXXX / XXXX				
• Other		XXXXXXXX / XXXX				
c) Consultants						
d) User Personnel		DOLLARS / HRS.		DOLLARS / HRS.		DOLLARS / HRS.
• Administrative/ Faculty						XXXXXXXX / XXXX
• Clerical						
• Technical						
	CODE	TOTAL DOLLARS	CODE	TOTAL DOLLARS	CODE	YEARLY DOLLARS
II. EQUIPMENT		$		$		$
III. SOFTWARE (purchased or leased)		XXXXXXXX XXXX		$		$
IV. SUPPLIES		$		$		$
V. TRAVEL EXPENSES		$		$		$
VI. OVERHEAD		$		$		$
	ABOVE DOLLARS FIGURES ARE IN _____ DOLLARS (year)		ABOVE DOLLARS FIGURES ARE IN _____ DOLLARS (year)		ABOVE DOLLARS FIGURES ARE IN _____ DOLLARS (year)	

DEFINITIONS FOR COST CHRONOLOGY

STAGES OF SYSTEM DEVELOPMENT AND OPERATION:

I. Definition - Includes: determination of information needs, feasibility study, examination of purchasable software, attendance at workshops, schools or conferences related to this procedure, and general system design. Probably will only involve administrative, technical and consulting personnel. A systems specification or its equivalent might usually result from this stage.

II. Development and Installation - Includes: detailed systems design, file and program design, writing and debugging of programs, writing procedures manuals, training costs, one time costs for purchased equipment and purchased programs. Costs associated with collection of data above and beyond that collected on a recurring basis. An operating program will usually be the result of this stage.

III. Operation and Maintenance - Includes: costs associated with program modifications, equipment usage, recurring costs such as yearly data preparation, machine time, operator time. These should be expressed in terms of one typical year (it is assumed that they will be fairly consistent from one year to the next).

COST CATEGORIES

I. Personnel - Personnel costs should all represent hours actually worked on this procedure. They should include any training and travel hours directly related to this procedure, but should not include vacation time, sick leave, etc. The dollar estimates should be estimates of the cost of the time shown.

    a. Producers - These are the people that actually produce the cost analysis information. In an automated system they will typically be the data processing staff (notice that the data capturers are in a separate category).

        ● Supervisory - includes time spent by the producer's management staff on this procedure.

        ● Technical - time spent by systems analysts, computer programmers, and others who would not be classified as clerical or supervisory.

        ● Clerical - includes time spent by secretaries, clerks, computer operators, etc.

    b. Capturers of Data - These are people who created and maintain the data files associated with this procedure. If a data file is used that already existed for another purpose then only include any hours spent in modifying it not the hours spent to initially collect it. This category may represent personnel from both the producers group and the users of the cost analysis information.

- Clerical - includes keypunchers, clerks who originally process source documents, secretaries, etc.

- Faculty - may be involved if procedure includes a faculty workload analysis. Should represent an estimate of average time to fill out multiplied by number of faculty sampled.

- Other - anyone else involved in data collection (in some instances this may be administrative personnel).

   c. <u>Consultants</u> - Includes time spent by consultants and charged to your organization. May include training, information analysis, systems analysis, program writing, etc.

   d. <u>User Personnel</u> - This category includes time spent by the user (user is the person or group that originally requested and/or will use the cost analysis information provided).

- Administrative - time spent by presidents, vice presidents, deans, budget officers, department chairmen, etc. Should not include time they spend using the information, only the time that they put in to help in its original development.

- Clerical - time spent by secretaries and clerks who work for the administrators mentioned above.

- Technical - time spent by non-managerial people who work for the user but who are at a higher functional level than is the clerical category.

II. <u>Equipment</u> - This includes equipment which was purchased or used for this procedure, equipment rental charges, storage charges, charge back cost from computer operations, a percentage of joint costs for "shared" equipment.

III. <u>Software</u> - This category only includes software purchased or leased from another source. If it involves a one time charge then it should be recorded in column two (Development and Installation), if it is a recurring annual charge, record it in column three (Operations).

IV. <u>Supplies</u> - This includes cost for paper, printing, magnetic tapes, disk packs, office supplies, etc.

V. <u>Travel Expenses</u> - Includes normal expenses, e.g., lodging, food, air fare, etc.; should not include wages or other paid to traveler, however.

VI. <u>Overhead</u> - Includes expenses for heat, electricity, space, insurance, and allocated administrative and secretarial costs.

APPENDIX 3

INSTITUTIONS SELECTED FOR SITE VISITS

Institution	Reasons for Choice[1]	Type[2]	Key[3] State
Wesleyan University Middletown, CT	Supposed successful SEARCH	2	
American University Washington, D.C.	Supposed difficulty PLANTRAN	2	
University of Bridgeport Bridgeport, CT	Supposed successful CAMPUS	2	
Texas Lutheran College Seguin, Texas	CASC computations Supposed Successful	4	
University of Pennsylvania Philadelphia, PA	Cost-income approach	4	
Purdue Lafayette, IN	Supposed successful NCHEMS	1	
North Dakota State School of Science Wahpeton, ND	Supposed highly successful NCHEMS	5	
University of Wisconsin- La Crosse La Crosse, WI	Supposed successful NCHEMS, Witmer	3	
California State University- Fullerton Fullerton, CA	Supposed difficulty NCHEMS	3	
Colby College Waterville, ME	Supposed difficulty CAMPUS	4	
Fisk University Nashville, TN	Supposed difficulty NCHEMS, own costing system	4	

---

[1] Probable success or difficulty as reported by developers of the systems.

[2] Refers to Carnegie type categories utilized in the study.

[3] The states were also selected for visits in key states listed.

APPENDIX 3

INSTITUTIONS SELECTED FOR SITE VISITS
(Continued)

Institution	Reasons for Choice[1]	Type[2]	Key[3] State
SUNY Plattsburg Plattsburg, NY	Supposed successful NCHEMS	3	NY
St. Petersburg Junior College St. Petersburg, FL	Supposed difficulty NCHEMS	5	FL
Westmar College Lemars, IA	Supposed successful PLANTRAN	4	
Seattle Community Colleges Seattle, WA	Supposed successful NCHEMS	5	WA
University of Michigan Ann Arbor, MI	Homemade System State PPB	1	MI
Coast Community College Costa Mesa, CA	Humanistic PPB NCHEMS Experience	5	
University of Toledo Toledo, OH	Supposed difficulty CAMPUS	3	OH
University of West Florida Pensacola, FL	Supposed difficulty NCHEMS	3	FL
University of Colorado Boulder, CO	Supposed difficulty CAMPUS	1	CO
University of Washington Seattle, WA	Homemade systems Experienced	1	WA

---

[1]Probable success or difficulty as reported by developers of the systems.

[2]Refers to Carnegie type categories utilized in the study.

[3]The states were also selected for visits in key states listed.

APPENDIX 4

CONDENSED STATE AGENCY INTERVIEW GUIDE

Outline

Section A. Background of Agency (see special sheet)

Section B. Background of Respondents (same as institutional form)

Section C. Agency Responsibility (see special sheet)

Section D. Budget Review--Non-formula

      I. Decision Process (or Subprocess) Description
     II. Description of Information Used in this Process (or Subprocess)
   III. Cost Information Not Obtained or Not Used
    IV. Detailed Cost Information Description
     V. Description of Cost Analysis Method Used
    VI. Evaluation of Cost Information/Analysis Method
   VII. Cost Information and Analysis Not Used (Rejected or Future)

Section E. Budget Review--Formula

    1. Decision process (as above)

Section F. Program Review

    1. Decision ... (as above)

Section G. Private College Contracts

    1. Decision ... (as above)

State of _____

Check one:

      ___ coordinating agency
      ___ governing board
      ___ legislative staff
      ___ budget office

Section A. Background of Agency

1. Identification

    Name   _____

    Location   _____

2. Documents   √ if we have

    Descriptions of authority (consti-
    tutional, legislative, executive)   _____

    Makeup of the board (if relevant:
    size, composition, term)   _____

    Description of budget review
    process (if relevant)   _____

    Description of budget formulas used   _____

    Copies of recurring and/or recent
    financial reports   _____

    Description of program review
    process (if relevant)   _____

    Description of any advisory committees
    involved in financial or cost analytic
    issues   _____

Section B

Background of Respondent (For each respondent interviewed)

Job Title_____   Name_____

As you know, administrators have widely varied backgrounds with respect to education and experience. We would like to get a clear picture of your background with respect to the following areas:

Degrees	Major	Location	Year
_____	_____	_____	_____
_____	_____	_____	_____
_____	_____	_____	_____
_____	_____	_____	_____

Would you please indicate the experience you have had in the following areas.

Type of Contact

Subjects	Courses	Short Courses	Extensive Reading	Job Experience
Institutional Research				
Accounting				
Management or Administration				
Operations Research or Management Science				
Economics				
Industrial Engineering				

In each box checked above, please make a numerical correspondence with the detailed description given below.

Please go back and explain the topics covered and the sources of the courses, readings, and job experience (type and how long).

Type of Contact

Specific Material	Short Courses	Extensive Reading	Job Experience
Resource Requirements Prediction Model (RRPM)			
Comprehensive Analytical Methods for Planning in University Systems (CAMPUS)			
System for Evaluating Alternative Commitments in Higher Education (SEARCH)			
Higher Education Long Range Planning/ Planning Translation (HELP/ PLANTRAN)			
National Center for Higher Education Management Information Systems' Information Exchange Procedure (NCHEMS-IEP)			
Program Classification Structure (PCS)			
Planning Programming Budgeting Systems (PPBS)			
Standard Costing			
Marginal Costing			
Cost Simulation Models			
Cost Accounting Models			

As you did before, please number the boxes to correspond with their description below.

Please go back and explain the topics covered and the sources of the courses, readings, and job experience (type and how long).

Section C. Agency Responsibility

1. Does your agency have responsibility of reviewing non-formula, operating budget requests and recommending appropriation levels for public institutions of higher education in your state?

    _____ Yes   _____ No

    [If "yes," go to Section D, page ___. Also, be certain that we have any pre-prepared documents describing the process.]

2. Does your agency have responsibility for establishing, adjusting, and analyzing the effects of, formulas used in budget requests by public higher education institutions in your state?

    _____ Yes   _____ No

    [If "yes," go to Section E, page ___. Also, be certain that we have any pre-prepared documents describing the process.]

3. Does your agency have responsibility for reviewing, and otherwise acting upon, institutional requests to establish new academic programs (degrees, majors, minors, certificate) and institutions or the disestablishment of programs and institutions?

    _____ Yes   _____ No

    [If "yes," go to Section F, page ___. Also, be certain that we have any pre-prepared documents describing the process.]

4. Does your agency have responsibility for operating a state program for providing support on a contractual basis to the state's private colleges or universities?

    _____ Yes   _____ No

    [If "yes," go to Section G, page ___. Also, be certain that we have any pre-prepared documents describing the process.]

Section D. Budget Review--Non-formula

Please concentrate on those responsibilities of your agency associated with the review of the non-formulary requests of state public institutions of higher education for operating expenses (for example, deciding on format for budget submissions, reviewing and analyzing justifications for budget request levels, and recommending appropriation levels).

Interviewee_____

Process (Subprocess)_____

QUESTIONS FOR EACH DECISION PROCESS OR SUBPROCESS

Part I.   Decision Process (or Subprocess) Description

How does this decision process (or subprocess) operate? Provide a brief description of who is involved, timing, procedures used, etc.

Part II.   Description of Information Used in this Decision Process (or Subprocess)

1. What types (cost and non-cost) of information are supplied by institutions and other sources to your agency in connection with this decision process?

a.   _____
b.   _____
c.   _____
d.   _____
e.   _____

2. What types (cost and non-cost) of information are used in this decision process (or subprocess)?

a.   _____
b.   _____
c.   _____
d.   _____
e.   _____

Please roughly rank the relative importance of these above types of information.

[NOTE to Interviewer: if cost data or cost information is not mentioned then go on to Part III.]

If cost information is mentioned ascertain whether it is actually used in the decision process (or subprocess). For example, if the interviewee evidences a high degree of familiarity with the cost information this possibly indicates that the cost information is actually used. If the cost information is not used then go on to Part III. If cost information is used, then go on to Part IV.

Part III. Cost Information Not Obtained or Not Used

    1. Why do you feel that the non-cost information is important in this decision process (or subprocess) and cost information is not?

    2. Was cost information for this decision process (or subprocess) ever obtained or used and subsequently dropped or rejected?
       _____ Yes   _____ No

If yes, what types of cost information were used or considered for this decision process (or subprocess)?

    a. _____

    b. _____

    c. _____

(Reference to producer system if possible.)

If yes, why were they dropped or rejected?

    3. What cost information do you think you want for use in this decision process (or subprocess)?

    a. _____

    b. _____

    c. _____

How would this cost information affect this decision process?

What problem do you expect or are you having in acquiring this cost information?

    4. In the next 3 to 5 years what changes (if any) in cost information relevant to this decision process (or subprocess) do you expect to occur? Please identify (if any) those which you want and those which you don't want.

[NOTE to Interviewer: do not fill out subsequent questions for this decision process (or subprocess). Go to the next decision process.]

Part IV. <u>Detailed Cost Information Description</u>

Generic cost name:_____
(from Part II)

<u>Description of Cost Information Type</u>

If a detailed description of system or procedure outputs has already been made, reference those output numbers that are actually used in the decision process. Use the same output numbers as recorded in the producer interviews. If a detailed description has not been previously made, fill out this section for cost information actually used.

Complete Parts IV-VI for each of the different systems or procedures recorded in Part II. Several iterations of Parts IV-VI may then be needed, if separate cost systems or procedures were recorded in Part II.

A. <u>Measure of Cost</u>   <u>Output Measure</u>

   ___ Total*   ___ Student Credit Hour

   ___ Average (per unit)   ___ Student Contact Hour

   ___ Marginal/Incremental   ___ FTE Student (Major)

                     ___ Headcount Students

  * no output measure required ___ Degree Granted

                     ___ Other _____

                     ___ Other _____

B. <u>Allocation</u>   <u>Allocation and Basis</u>

   ___ Direct   _____

   ___ Indirect (Allocated) _____

   ___ Full (Direct & Indirect) _____

                   (use reverse side if necessary)

C. Volume Relationship (If Identified)

___ Variable

___ Fixed

___ Semi-Variable or Mixed

D. Cost Basis

___ Historical Actual   ___ Replacement

___ Standard   ___ Imputed

___ Estimated (Projected) - basis of projection

                               ___ historical

                               ___ other _____

E. Subject of Costing

___ Organizational Unit (e.g., department, college, etc.)

___ Program (e.g., major, degree, research output)

___ Program/Function (e.g., instruction, research, service, etc.)

___ Activity (e.g., discipline, course, research project, scheduled teaching, advising)

___ Object of Cost (e.g., faculty salaries, supplies, etc.)

Description of each entry above:
(Identify by procedure number if there is more than one output; record a description for each output above)

_____

_____

_____

_____

_____

_____

F. Additional Descriptive Comments

_____

_____

_____

_____

- -

Part V. <u>Description of Cost Analysis Method Used</u>

5. Which of the following methods of cost <u>analysis</u> are used in this process. Record all analyses used, whether provided by producers or done by users themselves. Describe the method used. Identify types of data used in the analysis.

    a. percentages or ratios of cost elements.

    b. comparisons (over time perhaps) of cost against budget or standards or between institutions.

    c. comparisons of costs between decision alternatives.

    d. cost-volume analysis

    e. break-even analysis (cost-volume-revenue relationships).

    f. other

6. We want to separate those methods of cost analysis which are performed by users, such as yourself, from those methods which are provided by producers in finished form.

Identify [with a * above (in question 5)] those methods of cost analysis that are performed entirely or for the most part by users, after the information is transmitted to them.

Part VI. <u>Evaluation of Cost Information/Analysis Method</u>

In this part and the next part we are referring to the cost information and the cost analysis method combined. If the experience with the cost information differs from the experience with the analysis method, split your answers in each such questions.

7. Who determined the content and form of this cost information/ analysis method? Characterize role of producer versus user.

8. Briefly describe why this type of cost information/analysis method was selected?

9. Characterize the role of this cost information/analysis method in the decision process (or subprocess). What is the relative importance of the cost information and analysis <u>used</u> and what actual and potential impact does it have on this decision process (or subprocess)? Is it necessary?

10. What problems have been encountered in obtaining and using this cost information/analysis? (e.g., lack of producer knowledge, lack of user user knowledge, user resistance, timeliness, lack of funds, misuse of data).

11. Of these problems which were the most important to overcome?

12. Have these problems been overcome? If so, how? If not, why not?

    Go back to Part IV, if all cost systems or procedures originally listed in Part II have not been documented by Parts IV-VI.

Part VII. Cost Information and Analysis Not Used (Rejected or Future)

13. Was other cost information or cost analysis ever obtained or used for this decision process (or subprocess) and subsequently dropped or rejected? Y   N   (circle one)

    If yes, what types of other cost information or cost analysis methods were used or considered for this decision process (or subprocess)?

    a. _____

    b. _____

    c. _____

    If yes, why were they dropped or rejected?

14. Can you conceive of any other cost or cost analysis method which would actually be of use in this decision process (or subprocess)? Y   N   (circle one)

    If yes, what are they?

    a. _____

    b. _____

    c. _____

    If yes, how would this other cost information or analysis method affect this decision process?

    If yes, what problems do you expect in acquiring this other cost information/analysis?

15. In the next 3 to 5 years what changes (if any) in cost information or analysis relevant to this decision process (or subprocess) do you expect to occur? Please identify (if any) those which you want and those which you don't want.

APPENDIX 5

MAIL SURVEY DOCUMENTS

AMERICAN COUNCIL ON EDUCATION
ONE DUPONT CIRCLE
WASHINGTON, D. C. 20036

OFFICE OF THE PRESIDENT

You may know that the American Council on Education is sponsoring a two-year study of the use and utility of cost analysis in higher education, with support from the Ford Foundation. It is being conducted for ACE by a research group at the University of Minnesota under the direction of Dr. Carl R. Adams of the Department of Management Sciences. The main purpose of the study is to secure information that would enable institutions to respond more effectively to internal and external pressures for more efficient use of resources and improved accountability.

An intensive interview study has been completed through site visits to a sample of institutions. Based on the results of that study, the next phase of the project requires the gathering of information by a mail survey from a relatively large number of colleges and universities. The purpose of this letter is to invite your institution to participate.

Needless to say, I make this request with great reluctance, since I am acutely aware of the growing burden falling upon colleges and universities due to the increasing volume of questionnaires from governmental and other sources. By way of partial mitigation, however, I can say that we hope the results of this study will help to check or redirect prospective efforts to collect more extensive cost information from institutions than is needed.

The survey is presented in two parts, each addressed to a different type of administrative officer:

Questionnaire I, which requests factual information regarding the various types of cost information that might be available at your institution. A self-addressed, prepaid envelope is enclosed for the return of the completed questionnaire.

<u>Questionnaire II</u>, which requests evaluative responses regarding:
(a) the relative usefulness of different types of cost-related
(including unit-cost) data; (b) the relationship of unit-cost information to public appropriations for higher education; (c) state
and federal demands for cost information; (d) interinstitutional comparisons of cost data; (e) different types of costing systems. It
is hoped that Questionnaire II can be completed by a high-level academic officer at each institution, such as the provost, the vice
president for academic affairs, or the president. Your own responses
to the open-ended question in each section would be particularly
welcomed. A separate envelope, postage prepaid, is enclosed for
the return of Questionnaire II.

A summary of the results will be sent to all participants without identification of individual institutions. A copy of your responses might be kept,
therefore, for use in making comparisons with the aggregated data.

We shall be very grateful indeed for your institution's participation in
this survey.

Sincerely yours,

Roger W. Heyns
President

Staff Use Only

CARD 1

(1-6)

(6-10)

(11-13)

Questionnaire I

STUDY OF COST ANALYSIS IN HIGHER EDUCATION
737 BUSINESS ADMINISTRATION BUILDING
UNIVERSITY OF MINNESOTA
MINNEAPOLIS, MINNESOTA 55455

SURVEY OF COST-RELATED ACADEMIC DATA AND ANALYSIS
IN INSTITUTIONS OF HIGHER EDUCATION

The questions in this survey are designed to explore the following four topics **with regard to your institution:** A) academic data base; B) academic data computations: C) data and costing models, systems and concepts; and D) external demand for academic cost and cost-related information. **These questions pertain ONLY to data and analysis computed or aggregated at the institutional level** (i.e., data representing the entire institution rather than that generated in or for an individual department or other sub-unit unless similar data were generated for all such departments or sub-units).

Please answer each question by **circling** the appropriate response. **For many questions more than one response may be appropriate.** Only in questions 1 and 2 of Part D will you be asked to give a short written response. Leave blank any question for which you are uncertain of the answer.

You will note that many questions in Parts A and B refer to data recorded "by discipline." **In answering these questions, you may consider data recorded "by department" at your institution equivalent to data recorded "by discipline" IF most departments at your institution represent a single discipline. Please respond to the following statement.**

In responding to questions regarding data recorded or calculated "by discipline," I am substituting "by department."   YES (1)   NO (2)   (14)

When you have completed this questionnaire, please return it in the prepaid return envelope. Thank you for your help.

Part A. ACADEMIC DATA

1. Does your institution currently have the following academic data?

Circle the Appropriate Answer in Each Column

a. Enrollment

	CURRENT YEAR	LAST YEAR	2 YEARS BACK	CARD 1
headcount by student level (e.g., freshman or lower division)	YES (1) NO (2)	YES (1) NO (2)	YES (1) NO (2)	(15-17)
FTE by student level	YES (1) NO (2)	YES (1) NO (2)	YES (1) NO (2)	(18-20)
headcount by major (e.g., history)	YES (1) NO (2)	YES (1) NO (2)	YES (1) NO (2)	(21-23)
b. Degrees conferred by major	YES (1) NO (2)	YES (1) NO (2)	YES (1) NO (2)	(24-26)

c. Course enrollment

	CURRENT YEAR	LAST YEAR	2 YEARS BACK	
average headcount by discipline (e.g., French)	YES (1) NO (2)	YES (1) NO (2)	YES (1) NO (2)	(27-29)
average headcount by discipline and course level (e.g., upper division French)	YES (1) NO (2)	YES (1) NO (2)	YES (1) NO (2)	(30-32)

PLEASE CONTINUE ⟶

Circle the Appropriate Answer in Each Column

	CURRENT YEAR	LAST YEAR	2 YEARS BACK	
d. Student credit hours				
by discipline (e.g., English)	YES (1) NO (2)	YES (1) NO (2)	YES (1) NO (2)	(33-35)
by discipline and course level (e.g., lower division English)	YES (1) NO (2)	YES (1) NO (2)	YES (1) NO (2)	(36-38)
by discipline and student major (e.g., English taken by history majors)	YES (1) NO (2)	YES (1) NO (2)	YES (1) NO (2)	(39-41)
e. Number of faculty				
headcount by discipline	YES (1) NO (2)	YES (1) NO (2)	YES (1) NO (2)	(42-44)
FTE by discipline	YES (1) NO (2)	YES (1) NO (2)	YES (1) NO (2)	(45-47)
headcount by discipline and rank	YES (1) NO (2)	YES (1) NO (2)	YES (1) NO (2)	(48-50)
FTE by discipline and rank	YES (1) NO (2)	YES (1) NO (2)	YES (1) NO (2)	(51-53)
f. Faculty **instructional** load				
credit hours by discipline	YES (1) NO (2)	YES (1) NO (2)	YES (1) NO (2)	(54-56)
contact hours by discipline	YES (1) NO (2)	YES (1) NO (2)	YES (1) NO (2)	(57-59)
other _____ (60) (specify)	YES (1) NO (2)	YES (1) NO (2)	YES (1) NO (2)	(61-63)
credit hours by discipline and rank	YES (1) NO (2)	YES (1) NO (2)	YES (1) NO (2)	(64-66)
contact hours by discipline and rank	YES (1) NO (2)	YES (1) NO (2)	YES (1) NO (2)	(67-69)
other _____ (70) (specify)	YES (1) NO (2)	YES (1) NO (2)	YES (1) NO (2)	(71-73)
g. Faculty activity				
assigned load by discipline	YES (1) NO (2)	YES (1) NO (2)	YES (1) NO (2)	(74-76)
reported activity by discipline	YES (1) NO (2)	YES (1) NO (2)	YES (1) NO (2)	(77-79)
other _____ (10) (specify)	YES (1) NO (2)	YES (1) NO (2)	YES (1) NO (2)	CARD 2 (11-13)
h. Faculty salaries				
individual $ by discipline	YES (1) NO (2)	YES (1) NO (2)	YES (1) NO (2)	(14-16)
average $ by discipline	YES (1) NO (2)	YES (1) NO (2)	YES (1) NO (2)	(17-19)
individual $ by discipline and rank	YES (1) NO (2)	YES (1) NO (2)	YES (1) NO (2)	(20-22)
average $ by discipline and rank	YES (1) NO (2)	YES (1) NO (2)	YES (1) NO (2)	(23-25)

Circle the Appropriate Answer in Each Column

i. Tuition income

	CURRENT YEAR	LAST YEAR	2 YEARS BACK	
by discipline or student major	YES (1) NO (2)	YES (1) NO (2)	YES (1) NO (2)	(26-28)
by discipline or student major and student level	YES (1) NO (2)	YES (1) NO (2)	YES (1) NO (2)	(29-31)

Circle ONE Answer

	POOR	MARGINAL BUT USABLE	GOOD	EXCELLENT	
2. How do you rate the overall accuracy of your current data files?					
student data	1	2	3	4	(32)
faculty load/activity data	1	2	3	4	(33)
faculty salary data	1	2	3	4	(34)

Circle ALL APPROPRIATE Answers

	DO NOT HAVE	NOT MACHINE READABLE	PARTIALLY MACHINE READABLE	FULLY MACHINE READABLE	HAVE ON-LINE ACCESS	
3. Are your student data files machine readable						
course enrollment (headcount)	1	2	3	4	5	(35-36)
student credit hours	1	2	3	4	5	(37-38)
student records (student level and degrees conferred)	1	2	3	4	5	(39-40)
4. Are your faculty data files machine readable?						
faculty course assignment	1	2	3	4	5	(41-42)
instructional load	1	2	3	4	5	(43-44)
activity report	1	2	3	4	5	(45-46)
salaries	1	2	3	4	5	(47-48)

Circle ONE Answer

5. Are your files "keyed" to permit integration of the data?			
student registration data with faculty assignment data	YES (1)	NO (2)	(49)
faculty assignment data with salary data	YES (1)	NO (2)	(50)
6. Have your expenditure accounts been reclassified on the basis of the activities supported?	YES (1)	NO (2)	(51)

Part B. ACADEMIC DATA COMPUTATIONS

Circle the Appropriate Answer in Each Column

Does your institution currently have the following information?

	CURRENT YEAR		LAST YEAR		2 YEARS BACK		EXPECT TO HAVE NEXT YEAR		HIGH PRIORITY NEXT 2-5 YEARS		
1. Student credit hours per FTE faculty											
by discipline	1 YES	2 NO	1 YES	2 NO	1 YES	2 NO	1 YES	2 NO	1 YES	2 NO	(52-56)
by discipline and course level	1 YES	2 NO	1 YES	2 NO	1 YES	2 NO	1 YES	2 NO	1 YES	2 NO	(57-61)
by discipline and faculty rank	1 YES	2 NO	1 YES	2 NO	1 YES	2 NO	1 YES	2 NO	1 YES	2 NO	(62-66)

Circle the Appropriate Answer in Each Column

	CURRENT YEAR		LAST YEAR		2 YEARS BACK		EXPECT TO HAVE NEXT YEAR		HIGH PRIORITY NEXT 2-5 YEARS		CARD 3
2. FTE students per FTE faculty											
by discipline	1 YES	2 NO	1 YES	2 NO	1 YES	2 NO	1 YES	2 NO	1 YES	2 NO	(10-14)
by discipline and course level	1 YES	2 NO	1 YES	2 NO	1 YES	2 NO	1 YES	2 NO	1 YES	2 NO	(15-19)
by discipline and faculty rank	1 YES	2 NO	1 YES	2 NO	1 YES	2 NO	1 YES	2 NO	1 YES	2 NO	(20-24)
by discipline, faculty rank and course level	1 YES	2 NO	1 YES	2 NO	1 YES	2 NO	1 YES	2 NO	1 YES	2 NO	(25-29)
3. Direct instructional costs											
total by discipline	1 YES	2 NO	1 YES	2 NO	1 YES	2 NO	1 YES	2 NO	1 YES	2 NO	(30-34)
total by discipline and course level	1 YES	2 NO	1 YES	2 NO	1 YES	2 NO	1 YES	2 NO	1 YES	2 NO	(35-39)
total by individual course	1 YES	2 NO	1 YES	2 NO	1 YES	2 NO	1 YES	2 NO	1 YES	2 NO	(40-44)
average per SCH by discipline	1 YES	2 NO	1 YES	2 NO	1 YES	2 NO	1 YES	2 NO	1 YES	2 NO	(45-49)
average per SCH by discipline and course level	1 YES	2 NO	1 YES	2 NO	1 YES	2 NO	1 YES	2 NO	1 YES	2 NO	(50-54)
per SCH by individual course	1 YES	2 NO	1 YES	2 NO	1 YES	2 NO	1 YES	2 NO	1 YES	2 NO	(55-59)
average per student major by student level	1 YES	2 NO	1 YES	2 NO	1 YES	2 NO	1 YES	2 NO	1 YES	2 NO	(60-64)
average per degree recipient by major	1 YES	2 NO	1 YES	2 NO	1 YES	2 NO	1 YES	2 NO	1 YES	2 NO	(65-69)
4. Matrix of credit hours taken in each discipline by students in each major or other headcount descriptor (induced course load matrix)	1 YES	2 NO	1 YES	2 NO	1 YES	2 NO	1 YES	2 NO	1 YES	2 NO	(70-74)
5. Marginal costs (i.e., cost change caused by volume change) for instructional programs (not average unit costs)	1 YES	2 NO	1 YES	2 NO	1 YES	2 NO	1 YES	2 NO	1 YES	2 NO	(75-79)
											CARD 4
6. Ratios of tuition income to direct instructional costs by discipline	1 YES	2 NO	1 YES	2 NO	1 YES	2 NO	1 YES	2 NO	1 YES	2 NO	(10-14)
7. Allocations of indirect costs to instructional programs											
partial allocation	1 YES	2 NO	1 YES	2 NO	1 YES	2 NO	1 YES	2 NO	1 YES	2 NO	(15-19)
full allocation	1 YES	2 NO	1 YES	2 NO	1 YES	2 NO	1 YES	2 NO	1 YES	2 NO	(20-24)

PLEASE CONTINUE ⟶

Part C. DATA AND COSTING MODELS, SYSTEMS AND CONCEPTS

Circle ONE Answer

1. What experience has your institution had with each of the following?

Specific Models/Systems	NONE	ATTEMPTED BUT NEVER RUN	RUN IN THE PAST	CURRENTLY RUN	UNDER DEVELOPMENT	UNDER SERIOUS CONSIDERATION	WOULD LIKE TO TRY IT	
NCHEMS' RRPM	1	2	3	4	5	6	7	(25)
NCHEMS' IEP	1	2	3	4	5	6	7	(26)
HEPL/PLANTRAN	1	2	3	4	5	6	7	(27)
SEARCH	1	2	3	4	5	6	7	(28)
CAMPUS	1	2	3	4	5	6	7	(29)
other _____ (30)	1	2	3	4	5	6	7	(31)

Concepts

induced course load matrix	1	2	3	4	5	6	7	(32)
faculty activity analysis	1	2	3	4	5	6	7	(33)
enrollment projection modeling	1	2	3	4	5	6	7	(34)
revenue projection modeling	1	2	3	4	5	6	7	(35)

2. Answer the following for the **ONE** model, system or concept considered most significant in the experience of your institution.

Model, system or concept: _____ (specify) ( ) (36) STAFF USE

a. This model, system or concept was selected because of: **Circle ALL Appropriate Responses**

influence of top administrative officer(s)	1	(37-41)
influence of a staff member(s)	2	
requirements of the Board of Trustees	3	
requirements of a state agency	4	
influence of a consultant	5	
influence of the model/system's producer	6	
external funding made it possible	7	
other _____ (specify)	8	

PLEASE CONTINUE ⟶

180

Circle ALL Appropriate Answers

b. What difficulties were encountered in
developing (or installing) this model,
system, or concept

ENCOUNTERED / WAS ANTICIPATED / WAS OVERCOME

data base inaccuracies	1	2	3	(42-44)
data base not complete	1	2	3	(45-47)
data base not integrated	1	2	3	(48-50)
data difficult to access	1	2	3	(51-53)
cost	1	2	3	(54-56)
computer programming	1	2	3	(57-59)
lack of technical expertise	1	2	3	(60-62)
internal opposition	1	2	3	(63-65)

c. Was specific use(s) of the model, system or concept output
data determined before beginning the project?

YES (1)   NO (2)   PARTIALLY (3)   (66)

Part D. EXTERNAL DEMANDS FOR DATA AND INFORMATION ON COSTS AND COST VARIABLES.

1. Approximately how many man-days are required annually to
compile data for recovering indirect costs under research and
other grants?

Approximate Number of Annual Man-Days

from federal agencies	_____	(67-69)
from state agencies	_____	(70-72)
from private agencies	_____	(73-75)

2. Approximately how many man-days are required annually to
compile data on instructional costs or cost variables (e.g., class
size, teaching load, salaries) or to convert existing data for
reporting to the following external agencies?

Approximate Number of Annual Man-Days   CARD 5

Department of Health, Education and Welfare	_____	(10-12)
other federal agencies	_____	(13-15)
state educational board	_____	(16-18)
other state agencies	_____	(19-21)
accrediting associations	_____	(22-24)
consortia/voluntary associations	_____	(25-27)
other _____ (specify)	_____	(28-30)

3. What portion of the data supplied to all external agencies
is generated or compiled specifically for that purpose
(i.e., the data are not already available in some form)?

Circle ONE Answer

1 0-25%   2 26-50%   3 51-75%   4 76-100%   (31)

THANK YOU FOR YOUR COOPERATION. PLEASE RETURN THIS FORM IN THE PREPAID RETURN ENVELOPE.

Questionnaire II

STUDY OF COST ANALYSIS IN HIGHER EDUCATION
737 BUSINESS ADMINISTRATION BUILDING
UNIVERSITY OF MINNESOTA
MINNEAPOLIS, MINNESOTA 55455

**TOP ADMINISTRATORS' PERCEPTIONS REGARDING COST INFORMATION
AND COSTING SYSTEMS IN HIGHER EDUCATION**

This questionnaire consists of a series of statements regarding the use and usefulness of cost information in higher education, and experience with cost analysis systems in your institution. Your perception or attitude with regard to each statement should be recorded by **circling** the response you consider most appropriate. All the statements are written in a positive form so that no bias regarding the expected answer is implied.

Although most of the questions require categorical responses, a few open-ended questions have been included. Your answers to the open-ended questions will be especially helpful to the study. **When you have completed this questionnaire, please return it in the prepaid return envelope.** Thank you for your help.

Part A. In allocating funds to instructional departments or programs, you may use a variety of cost or cost-related data ranging from class size and faculty loads to cost per student credit hour (SCH) and cost per degree recipient. The following questions are intended to explore the various types of data used for instructional fund allocation decisions and the reasons underlying these data choices at your institution.

1. How important for decisions governing allocations of instructional funds **at your institution** are data on each of the following variables which may influence instructional costs?

Circle ONE Answer

	VERY IMPORTANT	IMPORTANT	LITTLE OR NO IMPORTANCE	DON'T KNOW	
a. average class size	1	2	3	4	(15)
b. faculty work load	1	2	3	4	(16)
c. student/faculty ratios	1	2	3	4	(17)
d. faculty salary scale	1	2	3	4	(18)
e. student credit hours (SCH) produced	1	2	3	4	(19)

2. How important for decisions governing allocations of instructional funds **at your institution** are each of the following types of unit cost data?

	VERY IMPORTANT	IMPORTANT	LITTLE OR NO IMPORTANCE	DON'T KNOW	
a. cost per SCH by discipline	1	2	3	4	(20)
b. cost per SCH by department	1	2	3	4	(21)
c. cost per degree granted	1	2	3	4	(22)
d. annual cost per student by major	1	2	3	4	(23)

3. Total costs of instruction and cost ratios (e.g., total cost of classroom instruction, ratios of supplies costs to instructional budget, percentage of instructional budget spent on computer use) are more important in the allocation of instructional funds **at your institution** than unit cost data (e.g., cost of instruction per SCH by discipline or annual cost of a student by major)

Circle ONE Answer

STRONGLY AGREE (1)	AGREE (2)	NEUTRAL (3)	DISAGREE (4)	STRONGLY DISAGREE (5)	DON'T KNOW (6)	(24)

4. Data related to factors influencing the costs of the instructional process (e.g., class size, faculty load, salary scale) are more important in the allocation of instructional funds **at your institution** than unit cost data (e.g., cost of instruction per SCH by discipline or annual cost of a student by major).

STRONGLY AGREE (1)	AGREE (2)	NEUTRAL (3)	DISAGREE (4)	STRONGLY DISAGREE (5)	DON'T KNOW (6)	(25)

PLEASE CONTINUE ⟶

5. Induced course load matrix data (i.e., the number of SCH taken in a discipline by students in each major) are useful in making instructional fund allocation decisions **at your institution.**

Circle ONE Answer

| STRONGLY AGREE (1) | AGREE (2) | NEUTRAL (3) | DISAGREE (4) | STRONGLY DISAGREE (5) | DON'T KNOW (6) | (26) |

6. Assuming that you have instructional unit cost data (e.g., cost of instruction per SCH by discipline or annual cost per student by major) **at your institution,** which of the following uses are served? **If you do not have instructional unit cost data, omit this question.**

Circle the Appropriate Answer

a. no direct use is made of the unit cost data		NOT USED (2)	(27)
b. to make allocation decisions	USED (1)	NOT USED (2)	(28)
c. to justify decisions already made	USED (1)	NOT USED (2)	(29)
d. to spot problem areas	USED (1)	NOT USED (2)	(30)
e. to increase your confidence in decision making	USED (1)	NOT USED (2)	(31)
f. to deal with potential criticisms	USED (1)	NOT USED (2)	(32)
g. to provide an image of good management	USED (1)	NOT USED (2)	(33)
h. other use: _____ (specify)	USED (1)		(34)

7. Please state your views on the **relative** usefulness of data related to the instructional process (e.g., class size, faculty workload, and student/faculty ratios) compared to unit cost data (e.g., cost of instruction per SCH by discipline or annual cost of a student by major) for the allocation of funds to instructional departments or programs. Why is one type of data more useful than another?

THIS SECTION SHOULD BE ANSWERED ONLY BY PUBLIC INSTITUTIONS. Private institutions should proceed to Part C.

Part B. Many states are beginning to require or already require submission of institutional data on unit costs of instruction (e.g., cost per SCH by discipline or annual cost per student by major). The questions in this section request your views on the desirability of utilizing such information as a basis for funding institutions through appropriations.

8. Your state legislature **should** begin or continue to strongly support institutional submission of instructional unit costs (e.g., cost per SCH by discipline or annual cost per student by major) to the state.

Circle ONE Answer

| STRONGLY AGREE (1) | AGREE (2) | NEUTRAL (3) | DISAGREE (4) | STRONGLY DISAGREE (5) | DON'T KNOW (6) | (35) |

9. The issues of economies of scale, stage of institutional development, program mix and separating research expenditures from instructional expenditures can be handled adequately in using instructional unit costs (e.g., cost per SCH by discipline or annual cost of a student by major) for appropriation decisions.

| STRONGLY AGREE (1) | AGREE (2) | NEUTRAL (3) | DISAGREE (4) | STRONGLY DISAGREE (5) | DON'T KNOW (6) | (36) |

10. Instructional unit cost data (e.g., cost per SCH by discipline or annual cost of a student per major) can be useful for developing a formula for distribution of state funds among institutions.

Circle ONE Answer

STRONGLY AGREE (1)   AGREE (2)   NEUTRAL (3)   DISAGREE (4)   STRONGLY DISAGREE (5)   DON'T KNOW (6)   (37)

11. State use of an instructional funding formula for public higher education
    a. decreases significantly the level of effort required for budget submissions.

STRONGLY AGREE (1)   AGREE (2)   NEUTRAL (3)   DISAGREE (4)   STRONGLY DISAGREE (5)   DON'T KNOW (6)   (38)

   b. tends to increase significantly the threat of detailed state control of institutions.

STRONGLY AGREE (1)   AGREE (2)   NEUTRAL (3)   DISAGREE (4)   STRONGLY DISAGREE (5)   DON'T KNOW (6)   (39)

   c. allows more time for institutional administrators to focus on internal management issues.

STRONGLY AGREE (1)   AGREE (2)   NEUTRAL (3)   DISAGREE (4)   STRONGLY DISAGREE (5)   DON'T KNOW (6)   (40)

   d. makes future appropriations more certain and thus facilitates longer range planning.

STRONGLY AGREE (1)   AGREE (2)   NEUTRAL (3)   DISAGREE (4)   STRONGLY DISAGREE (5)   DON'T KNOW (6)   (41)

   e. tends to direct the internal allocation of funds in a manner consistent with the formula allowances.

STRONGLY AGREE (1)   AGREE (2)   NEUTRAL (3)   DISAGREE (4)   STRONGLY DISAGREE (5)   DON'T KNOW (6)   (42)

12. Please indicate below the type of instructional unit cost data, if any, that you think is appropriate and useful for your state to request from your institution for appropriation purposes. Please address the level of detail that such cost information should reflect.

Part C. The demand for cost and budgetary information by state and federal agencies has increased. In this section, your views are requested on the appropriateness and the effects of these demands. **Exclude data submissions for recovery of indirect costs on grants, etc. from your considerations.** Both public and private institutions should respond.

13. The amount of cost and budgetary information demanded **of your institution** by state and federal agencies is within reason.

Circle ONE Answer

STRONGLY AGREE (1)   AGREE (2)   NEUTRAL (3)   DISAGREE (4)   STRONGLY DISAGREE (5)   DON'T KNOW (6)   (43)

14. The overall level of effort required **at your institution** to meet external demands for cost and budgetary information makes it very difficult to produce adequate cost infformation for internal decision making.

STRONGLY AGREE (1)   AGREE (2)   NEUTRAL (3)   DISAGREE (4)   STRONGLY DISAGREE (5)   DON'T KNOW (6)   (44)

15. State and federal agencies have a good idea of what cost information they need from your institution and how they can use it.

Circle ONE Answer

STRONGLY
AGREE (1)   AGREE (2)   NEUTRAL (3)   DISAGREE (4)   STRONGLY DISAGREE (5)   DON'T KNOW (6)   (45)

16. Cost information required by state and federal agencies is also useful for internal institutional decision making.

STRONGLY
AGREE (1)   AGREE (2)   NEUTRAL (3)   DISAGREE (4)   STRONGLY DISAGREE (5)   DON'T KNOW (6)   (46)

17. If you feel the demand for cost and budgetary information by state and federal agencies should be reduced, how can this be accomplished?

Part D. Some institutions have been involved in the exchange of cost and other data that might be useful for internal decision making. The questions below request your opinion on the usefulness of cost and cost-related data exchange and how it might be accomplished.

18. Instructional cost comparisons among institutions are useful for decisions regarding the allocation of funds to instructional departments and programs.

Circle ONE Answer

STRONGLY
AGREE (1)   AGREE (2)   NEUTRAL (3)   DISAGREE (4)   STRONGLY DISAGREE (5)   DON'T KNOW (6)   (47)

19. The NCHEMS Information Exchange Program (IEP) is sufficiently refined and definitive so that cost comparisons among programs could be meaningful for your institution.

STRONGLY
AGREE (1)   AGREE (2)   NEUTRAL (3)   DISAGREE (4)   STRONGLY DISAGREE (5)   DON'T KNOW (6)   (48)

20. Voluntary exchange of cost-related data (e.g., class sizes, faculty loads, student/faculty ratios) among selected schools would be useful to your institution.

STRONGLY
AGREE (1)   AGREE (2)   NEUTRAL (3)   DISAGREE (4)   STRONGLY DISAGREE (5)   DON'T KNOW (6)   (49)

21. Comparisons of cost and cost-related information among **selected** schools would be more valuable to your institution than comparison with national averages of the same cost and cost-related factors.

STRONGLY
AGREE (1)   AGREE (2)   NEUTRAL (3)   DISAGREE (4)   STRONGLY DISAGREE (5)   DON'T KNOW (6)   (50)

PLEASE CONTINUE ⟶

185

22. In a paragraph, please state below your views on the usefulness of exchange of cost information among institutions and the purposes that can be served by such exchange.

Part E. In this section, your evaluation of a costing system is requested. **IF YOUR INSTITUTION HAS NOT HAD EXPERIENCE WITH ONE OR MORE OF THESE SYSTEMS, OMIT THIS SECTION.** Examples of costing systems are IEP, CAMPUS, RRPM, SEARCH, or "homemade" systems. If your institution has had experience with more than one system, select the system with which you are most familiar for answering the following questions. The system to be described is: _____

_____ (51)
(specify)

23. What is the current operational status of this system?

	Circle ONE Answer	
a. never reached fully operational status	1	(52)
b. reached operational status but is no longer being run	2	
c. currently in an operational status	3	

24. This costing system was selected because of: **Circle the Appropriate Answers**

a. influence of top administrative officer(s)	YES (1)	NO (2)	(53)
b. influence of a staff member(s)	YES (1)	NO (2)	(54)
c. request/directive of the Board of Trustees	YES (1)	NO (2)	(55)
d. requirement of a state agency	YES (1)	NO (2)	(56)
e. influence of a consultant	YES (1)	NO (2)	(57)
f. influence of the system's producer	YES (1)	NO (2)	(58)
g. external funding made it possible	YES (1)	NO (2)	(59)

25. Difficulties encountered in developing (or installing) this system were:

a. none significant	YES (1)	NO (2)	(60)
b. inadequate input data available	YES (1)	NO (2)	(61)
c. insufficient funds available	YES (1)	NO (2)	(62)
d. computer programming difficulties	YES (1)	NO (2)	(63)
e. lack of technical expertise	YES (1)	NO (2)	(64)
f. lack of administrative support	YES (1)	NO (2)	(65)
g. user resistance to using system outputs	YES (1)	NO (2)	(66)

26. Most of the difficulties encountered were anticipated.

Circle ONE Answer

STRONGLY
AGREE (1)   AGREE (2)   NEUTRAL (3)   DISAGREE (4)   STRONGLY
DISAGREE (5)   DON'T
KNOW (6)   (67)

27. This system has produced useful information for decision making within your institution.

STRONGLY
AGREE (1)   AGREE (2)   NEUTRAL (3)   DISAGREE (4)   STRONGLY
DISAGREE (5)   DON'T
KNOW (6)   (68)

28. This system will eventually produce useful information for decision making within your institution.

STRONGLY
AGREE (1)   AGREE (2)   NEUTRAL (3)   DISAGREE (4)   STRONGLY
DISAGREE (5)   DON'T
KNOW (6)   (69)

29. Have the system and its outputs been useful to your institution in any of the following ways?

Circle the Appropriate Answers

a. day-to-day institutional management	YES (1) NO (2)	(70)
b. long range planning	YES (1) NO (2)	(71)
c. better integration of institutional data	YES (1) NO (2)	(72)
d. better data for external inquiries	YES (1) NO (2)	(73)
e. better information for allocation of resources	YES (1) NO (2)	(74)
f. forecasting	YES (1) NO (2)	(75)

30. The benefits to your institution have outweighed the costs of this system.

Circle ONE Answer

STRONGLY
AGREE (1)   AGREE (2)   NEUTRAL (3)   DISAGREE (4)   STRONGLY
DISAGREE (5)   DON'T
KNOW (6)   (76)

31. A greater involvement on the part of administrators would have been beneficial in the selection and design of this costing system.

STRONGLY
AGREE (1)   AGREE (2)   NEUTRAL (3)   DISAGREE (4)   STRONGLY
DISAGREE (5)   DON'T
KNOW (6)   (77)

32. Briefly state your views on the usefulness of this costing system to your institution. Please identify particular benefits that have been realized.

THANK YOU FOR YOUR COOPERATION. PLEASE RETURN THIS FORM IN THE PREPAID RETURN ENVELOPE.

AMERICAN COUNCIL ON EDUCATION

J. W. Peltason, President

The American Council on Education, founded in 1918 and
composed of institutions of higher education and national
and regional education associations, is the nation's major
coordinating body for postsecondary education. Through
voluntary and cooperative action, the Council provides comprehensive leadership for improving educational standards,
policies, and services.